NGER GAMES TO THE BIG SCREEN? WHO INVENTED FACEBOOK? WHO BECAME THE COUNTRY
IO BECAME AN INTERNATIONAL HERO AT THE 1936 BERLIN GAMES? WHO CREATED A CODE THAT H
THE BOY BAND THAT ROSE TO FAME ON REALITY TV? WHO WAS A LE PEOPL
EE"? WHO WERE THE JOURNALISTS WHO UNCOVERED THE WATERG S THE
VIRONMENTAL MOVEMENT? WHO CREATED SPIDER-MAN AND THE HULK? WHO INVENTED THE M
SKETBALL PHENOM KNOWN AS KING JAMES? WHO BUILT THE WORLD'S FIRST SUCCESSFUL AIRF
PEOPLE TO CLIMB TO THE TOP OF MOUNT EVEREST? WHOSE REFUSAL TO CHANGE SEATS CHANG
NOBEL PEACE PRIZE FOR HER CHARITY WORK IN INDIA? WHO WAS THE FIRST AMERICAN TO ORB
O IS THE MUSICIAN CREDITED WITH ORGANIZING THE LIVE AID CONCERTS? WHO WAS THE FIRST W
T? WHO WAS THE TOP-EARNING FEMALE RECORDING ARTIST OF 2014? WHO WAS THE ONLY WOM
D ALONE FOR A NEWSPAPER ASSIGNMENT? WHO WAS KNOWN AS THE QUEEN OF JAZZ? WHO WA
VE WON MORE THAN 25 GRAND SLAM TITLES? WHO HELPED AMERICANS MASTER THE ART OF F
SS KNOWN FOR HER HUMANITARIAN WORK? WHO DISCOVERED AND DEVELOPED PENICILLIN? WH
S THE FIRST PERSON TO RUN A FOUR-MINUTE MILE? WHO LED INDIA'S FIGHT FOR INDEPENDENCE
TIST BEST KNOWN FOR HER WORK WITH CHIMPANZEES? WHO BECAME THE FIRST AFRICAN-AME
IO LED THE CHICAGO BULLS TO SIX NBA CHAMPIONSHIPS? WHO WAS THE FIRST HISPANIC U.S. SU
HELIX STRUCTURE OF DNA? WHO IS THE MOST DECORATED OLYMPIAN? WHO PULLED OFF THE M
N GIVES NEARLY $4 BILLION TO CHARITY EACH YEAR? WHO IS THE SMALL-TOWN GIRL WHO BECAM
R BARRIER? WHO WAS THE OLDEST ELECTED U.S. PRESIDENT? WHO ROSE TO FAME ON THE TV
VHO WERE THE MOST DECORATED INFANTRYMEN IN U.S. HISTORY? WHO IS REGARDED AS THE GRE
MICKEY MOUSE? WHO WAS ONE OF THE MOST INFLUENTIAL ARCHITECTS OF THE 20TH CENTURY?
WOMEN'S RIGHTS IN THE 1960S AND 1970S? WHO WAS THE U.S. PRESIDENT WHO NEGOTIATED A
O HELPED GET RID OF POLIO? WHO IS THE WORLD'S MOST FAMOUS PIGEON? WHO WAS THE ME
VAS THE CELEBRATED CIVIL-RIGHTS ACTIVIST WHO WROTE I KNOW WHY THE CAGED BIRD SINGS?
THE ONLY U.S. PRESIDENT TO SERVE FOUR TERMS IN OFFICE? WHO IS THE ACCLAIMED AUTHOR
ON THE MOST NFL MVP AWARDS? WHO WAS THE PILOT WHO LANDED SAFELY IN THE HUDSON RI
AS THE IRON LADY? WHO HELPED BRING THE HUNGER GAMES TO THE BIG SCREEN? WHO INV
APPLE AND TRANSFORMED THE DIGITAL WORLD? WHO BECAME AN INTERNATIONAL HERO AT TH
WOMAN TO FLY SOLO ACROSS THE ATLANTIC? WHO IS THE BOY BAND THAT ROSE TO FAME ON R
E COULD "FLOAT LIKE A BUTTERFLY, STING LIKE A BEE"? WHO WERE THE JOURNALISTS WHO UNCO
ON? WHOSE BOOK LAUNCHED THE MODERN ENVIRONMENTAL MOVEMENT? WHO CREATED SPIDE
E 4 BY IMPERSONATING ELVIS? WHO BUILT THE WORLD'S FIRST SUCCESSFUL AIRPLANE? WHO
ER DIARY WAS PUBLISHED? WHO WERE THE FIRST PEOPLE TO CLIMB TO THE TOP OF MOUNT EVE
D JAWS, E.T., AND INDIANA JONES? WHO WON THE NOBEL PRIZE FOR HER CHARITY WORK IN INDIA
U.S. WOMEN'S SOCCER ON THE MAP? WHO IS THE MUSICIAN CREDITED WITH ORGANIZING THE LI
SHIP SHAPED THE CIVIL-RIGHTS MOVEMENT? WHO WAS THE TOP-EARNING FEMALE RECORDING
VAT? WHO TRAVELED AROUND THE WORLD ALONE FOR A NEWSPAPER ASSIGNMENT? WHO WAS K
ARE THE TENNIS-STAR SISTERS WHO HAVE WON MORE THAN 25 GRAND SLAM TITLES? WHO H
POPE? WHO IS THE HOLLYWOOD ACTRESS KNOWN FOR HER HUMANITARIAN WORK? WHO DISCO
DIVIDUAL ALL-AROUND EVENT? WHO WAS THE FIRST PERSON TO RUN A FOUR-MINUTE MILE? WH
G OF ROCK 'N' ROLL? WHO IS THE SCIENTIST BEST KNOWN FOR HER WORK WITH CHIMPANZEES?
ELOPED THE THEORY OF RELATIVITY? WHO LED THE CHICAGO BULLS TO SIX NBA CHAMPIONSHIPS
WAR II? WHO DISCOVERED THE DOUBLE-HELIX STRUCTURE OF DNA? WHO IS THE MOST DECO

BIG BOOK OF WHO

BIG BOOK OF WHO

TIME For Kids

Managing Editor Nellie Gonzalez Cutler
Creative Director Jennifer Kraemer-Smith
Project Editor Andrea Delbanco
Photo Editor Nataki Hewling
Copy Editor Heather Price-Wright

Created by 10Ten Media

Managing Directors Bob Der, Scott Gramling, Ian Knowles
Creative Director Crhistian Rodriguez
Managing Editor Andrea Woo
Writer Vickie An
Art Director Christine Capuano

Time Inc. Books

Publisher Margot Schupf
Vice President, Finance Vandana Patel
Executive Director, Marketing Services Carol Pittard
Executive Director, Business Development Suzanne Albert
Executive Director, Marketing Susan Hettleman
Executive Publishing Director Megan Pearlman
Associate Director of Publicity Courtney Greenhalgh
Assistant General Counsel Simone Procas
Assistant Director, Special Sales Ilene Schreider
Assistant Director, Finance Christine Font
Assistant Production Director Susan Chodakiewicz
Senior Manager, Sales Marketing Danielle Costa
Senior Manager, Children's Category Marketing Amanda Lipnick
Manager, Business Development and Partnerships Stephanie Braga
Associate Prepress Manager Alex Voznesenskiy

Editorial Director Stephen Koepp
Art Director Gary Stewart
Senior Editors Roe D'Angelo, Alyssa Smith
Managing Editor Matt DeMazza
Editor, Children's Books Jonathan White
Copy Chief Rina Bander
Design Manager Anne-Michelle Gallero
Assistant Managing Editor Gina Scauzillo
Editorial Assistant Courtney Mifsud

Special thanks: Allyson Angle, Keith Aurelio, Katherine Barnet, Brad Beatson, Jeremy Biloon, Ian Chin, Rose Cirrincione, Pat Datta, Assu Etsubneh, Alison Foster, Erika Hawxhurst, Kristina Jutzi, David Kahn, Jean Kennedy, Hillary Leary, Samantha Long, Kimberly Marshall, Robert Martells, Nina Mistry, Melissa Presti, Danielle Prielipp, Kate Roncinske, Babette Ross, Dave Rozzelle, Matthew Ryan, Ricardo Santiago, Divyam Shrivastava

For information on TIME FOR KIDS magazine for the classroom or home, go to TIMEFORKIDS.COM or call 800-777-8600.
For subscriptions to SI KIDS, go to SIKIDS.COM or call 800-889-6007.

Published by TIME FOR KIDS Books,
An imprint of Time Inc. Books
1271 Avenue of the Americas, 6th floor
New York, NY 10020

ISBN 10: 1-60320-245-5
ISBN 13: 978-1-60320-245-9
Library of Congress Control Number: 2015934214

We welcome your comments and suggestions about TIME FOR KIDS Books. Please write to us at: TIME FOR KIDS Books, Attention: Book Editors, P.O. Box 361095, Des Moines, IA 50336-1095
If you would like to order any of our hardcover Collector's Edition books, please call us at 800-327-6388, Monday through Friday, 7 a.m.–9 p.m. Central Time.

1 QGT 15

Welcome

• Who were the first people to get to the top of Mount Everest? Who was the only U.S. president to serve four terms in office? Who was the first woman to run a major television studio? Learn about these important figures—past and present—and all their amazing accomplishments in this book.

TIME For Kids presents more than 100 people you need to know, from brilliant scientists to chart-topping musicians, all-star athletes to powerful leaders. Learn all about the people who have shaped our world.

Contents

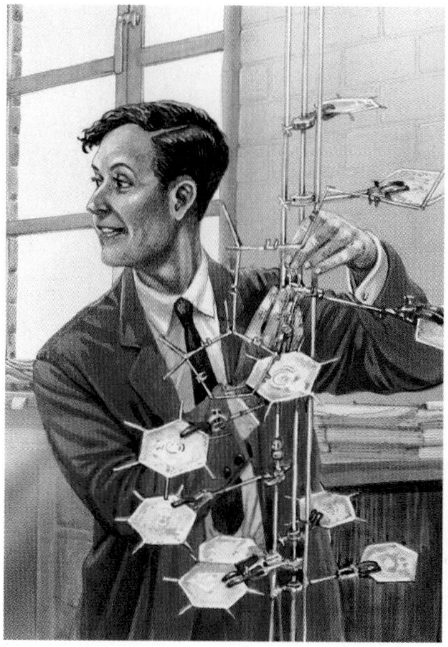

Groundbreakers

and Pioneers

Who were the first people to walk on the moon?

"That's one small step for a man, one giant leap for mankind." Astronaut **Neil Armstrong** said these famous words on July 20, 1969, the day he became the first person to set foot on the moon.

Armstrong and his fellow astronauts **Buzz Aldrin** and **Michael Collins** manned NASA's Apollo 11 mission. It was the U.S. space agency's first lunar landing mission. On July 16, the three-man crew blasted off into space inside the command module, called *Columbia*, from Kennedy Space ▶

● Aldrin exits the *Eagle* lunar module on July 20, 1969.

Aldrin stands next to the American flag he and Armstrong planted on the moon.

Center, in Cape Canaveral, Florida. Four days later, they were orbiting the moon. They were about to make history.

On the morning of July 20, Armstrong and Aldrin crawled into the *Eagle* lunar module. The smaller space-craft was connected to *Columbia*. They would pilot it to the moon's surface. Collins remained in orbit aboard *Columbia*.

Hours later, at 4:18 p.m., NASA's Mission Control, in Houston, Texas, received a radio call from Armstrong. "Houston, Tranquility Base here," he said. "The *Eagle* has landed." They had touched down on the moon!

Back on Earth, more than half a billion people watched the extraordinary event on television. At 10:56 p.m., Armstrong climbed down *Eagle*'s ladder and planted his feet on the ground. Aldrin followed shortly after.

The pair spent two and a half hours taking photos, setting up experiments, and collecting rock samples. With its mission complete, the crew returned safely to Earth on July 24. The triumph of the Apollo 11 mission paved the way for five more successful manned lunar landings. ■

Who was the first person to run a four-minute mile?

On the day **Roger Bannister** became the first person to run one mile in less than four minutes, he had considered canceling his attempt. It was rainy and windy on Iffley Road track, in Oxford, England. But the 25-year-old British medical student knew if he didn't try, someone else might beat him to it.

On May 6, 1954, with about 3,000 people watching, Bannister began his sprint into the record books. He had planned out the race very carefully. Two runners, Chris Brasher and Chris Chataway, helped him keep his pace. The crowd held its collective breath as Bannister burst down the final stretch. When he crossed the finish line, he nearly collapsed in exhaustion. Had he clocked in at under four minutes?

The answer was a resounding yes! Bannister made history that day with a time of three minutes and 59.4 seconds. ■

Who was the first Hispanic U.S. Supreme Court justice?

On August 8, 2009, **Sonia Sotomayor** was formally sworn in as the 111th U.S. Supreme Court justice. She was only the third woman to serve on the nation's highest court in 220 years. She was also the first Hispanic American.

Since taking her seat, Sotomayor has weighed in on many important issues, including campaign finance and health-care reform.

Sotomayor's passion for law began at an early age. She says watching the TV show Perry Mason inspired her to become a lawyer. She worked as an attorney and a judge, but says she never dreamed that she would one day sit on the U.S. Supreme Court.

"It is our nation's faith in a more perfect union that allows a Puerto Rican girl from the Bronx to stand here now," she said after being sworn in. "I am struck again by the wonder of my own life and the life we in America are so privileged to lead." ■

Who became the country's first female self-made millionaire?

Madam C.J. Walker is widely recognized as the nation's first self-made female millionaire. When Walker began suffering from a scalp ailment that caused her hair to fall out, she started to experiment with home remedies and store-bought products. In 1905, she came up with the perfect formula, which she called Wonderful Hair Grower. Walker decided to take a leap and start her own hair-care company, gearing the business to the needs of black women. By 1916, she had moved to New York City, and business was booming. She expanded her line, selling her products across the U.S. and the world. "I had to make my own living and my own opportunity," Walker once said. "But I made it! Don't sit down and wait for the opportunities to come. Get up and make them." ■

Who was known as the Queen of Jazz?

With her soulful voice and trademark improvisations, jazz singer **Ella Fitzgerald** knew how to make beautiful music. That's why she was known as the Queen of Jazz.

Fitzgerald was born on April 25, 1917, in Newport News, Virginia, and raised in Yonkers, New York. Growing up, she enjoyed playing baseball and dancing and singing with friends. Sometimes, they would take the train to Harlem, in New York City, to see shows at the legendary Apollo Theater.

It was there that the world first heard Fitzgerald. In 1934, her name was pulled from a weekly drawing to compete in Apollo's Amateur Night. She sang Hoagy Carmichael's "Judy" and the crowd went wild. That night, a star was born.

Fitzgerald was shy and reserved, but lit up in the spotlight. "Once up there, I felt the acceptance and love from my audience," Fitzgerald said. "I knew I wanted to sing [for] people [for] the rest of my life."

During a career that spanned six decades, Fitzgerald worked with greats including Louis Armstrong, Duke Ellington, and Frank Sinatra. By the 1990s, she had recorded more than 200 albums, sold more than 40 million copies of them, and won 13 Grammys. She was the first African-American woman to win the music industry's top prize. In 1991, the legendary singer gave her final performance, at New York's famed Carnegie Hall. ■

Who was the first woman to fly solo across the Atlantic?

People already knew **Amelia Earhart** before she became the first female pilot to fly across the Atlantic Ocean in 1932. Four years earlier, Earhart was the first woman passenger on a plane that crossed the Atlantic Ocean. People all over the world celebrated her accomplishment. But Earhart didn't see the flight as an achievement of her own. "I was just baggage, like a sack of potatoes," she said. She vowed to change that.

Earhart was already a pilot at the time. A trip to an air show in 1920 had sparked her interest in flying. Before long, she was taking flying lessons from a pioneering female aviator, Anita "Neta" Snook. In 1923, Earhart be-

came the 16th woman in the world to earn an international pilot's license.

After her famed passenger flight, Earhart set her sights on flying across the Atlantic again. But this time, she wanted to be in the pilot's seat, and she wanted to make the journey alone.

May 20, 1932, marked the fifth anniversary of American aviator Charles Lindbergh's famous flight across the Atlantic. On that day, Earhart took off from Harbour Grace, Newfoundland, to make history of her own. Fifteen hours later, on May 21, she landed in Londonderry, Northern Ireland. She had done it!

Soon after, she made another solo trip, from California to Hawaii. With this flight, ▶

► she became the first person to fly solo across both the Atlantic and Pacific Oceans.

Earhart's successes and spirit of adventure made her an international hero. She hoped her fame would open doors for other women pilots.

In 1937, Earhart prepared to make her biggest trip yet: a flight around the world. The journey would include many stops. In June, she and navigator Fred Noonan set off from Miami, Florida. Sadly, their plane disappeared on July 2, after leaving Papua New Guinea, an island in the South Pacific, north of Australia. The pair had been on their way to Howland Island, a small strip of land in the Pacific Ocean. The wreckage of their plane was never found.

Countless searches have been conducted on islands near where they vanished.

Artifacts such as tools, clothes, and metal pieces that may have been from Earhart's plane have been found. Could they have survived? It's still a mystery. But Earhart's bravery continues to inspire aviators everywhere. ■

You Should Also Know ...

Bessie Coleman, daredevil pilot

• Bessie Coleman was the world's first African-American female pilot, and the first black woman to stage a public flight in the United States. Because of gender and racial discrimination at the time in America, she moved to France to attend flying school and earn her pilot's license.

Coleman's specialties were stunt flying and parachuting. She never failed to wow audiences with her high-flying aerial tricks. But on April 30, 1926, while Coleman was preparing for an air show, something went tragically wrong. The 34-year-old pilot died in the accident.

A pioneer for women in aviation, the daring Coleman has not been forgotten. A postal stamp was issued in her honor in 1995.

Who helped Americans master the art of French cooking?

When many people think of French cooking, they picture American chef **Julia Child**. Why? The world-renowned TV personality and author is known for helping everyday home cooks master fancy French dishes.

Child moved to Paris with her husband in 1948. While there, she fell in love with the local cuisine. "After one taste of French food . . . I was hooked," she said. "The wonderful attention paid to each detail of the meal was incredible to me." She had discovered her true passion.

She started training at the world-famous Le Cordon Bleu cooking school, as well as under master chef Max Bugnard. After finishing the course, Child and two French friends founded their own school, the School of the Three Gourmands.

French cooking can be very complicated. Child and her partners worked to simplify the cuisine so that more people could prepare it. In 1961, after a decade of writing and research, they released *Mastering the Art of French Cooking*. The book achieved success almost immediately and is a classic in the culinary community.

A year after the 734-page book was published, Child headlined her own cooking show. *The French Chef* premiered locally in 1962 on WGBH, Boston's public broadcasting station. Child's humor, enthusiasm, and willingness to "make a mess" in the kitchen drew viewers in. Before long, TV stations across the country were airing the popular series. Child was a star!

More television programs and cookbooks would follow in her 40-year career. In 1993, she became the first woman inducted into the Culinary Institute of America's Hall of Fame. Child was also honored with numerous awards, including the Presidential Medal of Freedom in 2003.

The chef once said: "I don't think about whether people will remember me or not. I've been an okay person. I've learned a lot. I've taught people a thing or two. That's what's important." The world is still thanking her for it. ■

Who were the first people to climb to the top of Mount Everest?

In 1953, New Zealand explorer **Edmund Hillary** and his experienced guide **Tenzing Norgay** did what some thought was impossible. They climbed to the top of Earth's highest peak: Mount Everest.

The mighty mountain sits on the border between Nepal and China's Tibet region, in the Himalayas. Though people had previously attempted to reach Everest's 29,035-foot summit, none had succeeded, and many had died trying.

The climbing partners were part of an expedition led by the Royal Geographic Society. The team included a dozen climbers, 35 Sherpa guides, and 350 porters to transport

Hillary shot this photo of Norgay at the summit of Mount Everest.

supplies. They carried 18 tons of food and equipment for the two-month journey.

On May 26, 1953, one of the expedition's climbing teams failed in its attempt to reach the summit. Hillary and Norgay tried next. Two days later, the men set up their final camp and prepared for the historic ascent. The journey would be tough. They faced a dangerous, steep climb and icy conditions. But at 11:30 a.m. on May 29, they achieved their goal: They stood on top of the world!

Hillary took out his camera and snapped a photo of Norgay standing at the summit. In the famous picture, the Nepalese mountaineer is holding his ice pick and the flags of Nepal, Great Britain, India, and the United Nations. Before their descent, Norgay dug a hole in the snow and left an offering of candy, a chocolate bar, and some biscuits. Hillary dug a second hole and buried a cross. Fifteen minutes after arriving, they began their descent.

Hillary's zeal for adventure didn't end at the top of Everest. The renowned explorer went on to accomplish more amazing feats, including becoming the first person to reach the South Pole by motorized vehicle, in 1958.

To honor the Sherpa guides who had helped him summit Everest, Hillary founded the Himalayan Trust. Since 1960, the organization has been dedicated to bettering the lives of Nepalese people.

Thousands have since scaled Everest, including Hillary's son Peter, who did it in 1990. "Both Tenzing and I thought that once we'd climbed the mountain, it was unlikely anyone would ever make another attempt," Hillary later told *National Geographic Adventure*. "We couldn't have been more wrong." ■

Who was the first African American to win the U.S. Open and Wimbledon?

Much like Jackie Robinson was a pioneer for African Americans in baseball, **Arthur Ashe** paved the way in tennis. During his remarkable career, the tennis legend achieved many firsts. The most notable was in 1968, when he became the first male African-American tennis player to win a Grand Slam title, at the U.S. Open.

In 1970, Ashe made history again as the first African American to win the Australian Open. In 1975, he defeated Jimmy Connors to become the first black player to win Wimbledon.

Ashe discovered his knack for the game at a young age. The future sports star picked up his first racket at a neighborhood court when he was only 7 years old. As a teen, Ashe smashed the competition at the junior level. His talent earned him a college scholarship to UCLA, where he continued to dominate the

Ashe celebrates his first Grand Slam title at the U.S. Open in 1968.

sport, leading to his historic U.S. Open win. During his career, Ashe captured 33 singles titles and 14 doubles titles. He was inducted into the International Tennis Hall of Fame in 1985.

Ashe was a hero off the court, too. Throughout his life, the tennis champ was committed to helping underprivileged children. He helped create inner city tennis programs for youth, and cofounded what is today the National Junior Tennis and Learning Network. The organization is dedicated to developing kids' character through tennis and education.

Ashe used his fame to speak out about a number of political issues. He also sought to raise awareness ▶

Ashe poses with a child from Easter Seals, an organization that supports people with disabilities, in 1977.

about health issues such as heart disease and HIV/AIDS. Both plagued him in his later years, leading to his death in 1993, at the age of 49.

After his death, Ashe was awarded the Presidential Medal of Freedom by President Bill Clinton. Arthur Ashe Kids' Day is held in his honor at the start of the U.S. Open each year. The main stadium at the USTA Tennis Center, in Flushing, New York, the site of the U.S. Open, is named after the tennis legend ■

You Should Also Know . . .

Billie Jean King, tennis hero

Tennis legend Billie Jean King left her mark on the game and the world. During her career in the 1960s and 1970s, she won 39 Grand Slam singles, doubles, and mixed doubles titles.

King is also known for her work championing gender equality. She fought for equal prize money for female players and famously played men's champion Bobby Riggs in the Battle of the Sexes match in 1973. King crushed Riggs 6–4, 6–3, 6–3.

King's push for social change and equality forever impacted the way people view women in sports.

Who was the first woman to own and produce her own talk show?

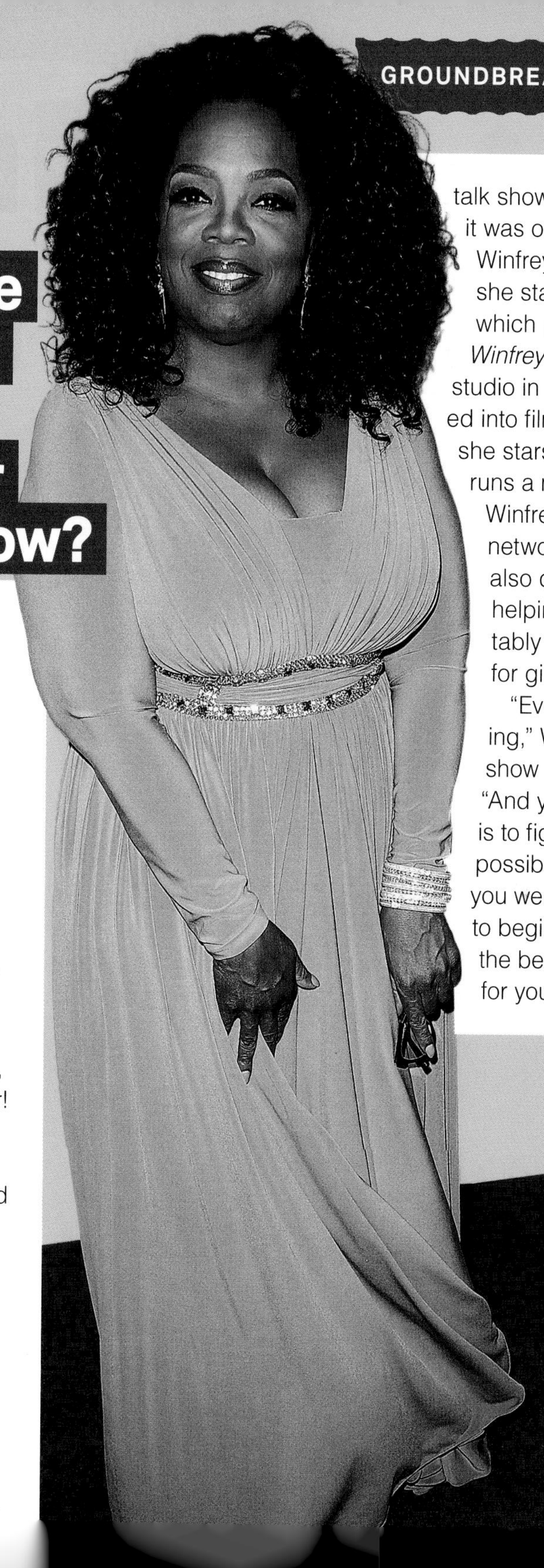

Oprah Winfrey, who is best known for hosting and producing a popular daytime talk show, is a self-made media tycoon—and one of the most respected people in entertainment.

Winfrey's broadcasting career began in high school, at a local radio station in Nashville, Tennessee. In 1976, she became a TV news anchor in Baltimore, Maryland, where she hosted her first talk show, *People Are Talking*. Pretty soon, people *were* talking—about her!

A few years later, Winfrey moved to Chicago, Illinois, to host a morning talk show called *AM Chicago*. In less than a month, the ratings began to soar. Viewers loved her warm and casual hosting style.

Soon the show was renamed *The Oprah Winfrey Show*. It was airing nationwide by 1986 and went on to become the highest-rated talk show in history. But it was only one piece of Winfrey's empire. In 1988, she started Harpo Studios, which produced *The Oprah Winfrey Show*. With her own studio in place, she expanded into film production. Today, she stars in movies and runs a magazine. In 2011, Winfrey launched a TV network, OWN. She has also dedicated her life to helping others, most notably by starting a school for girls in South Africa.

"Everybody has a calling," Winfrey said on her show *Oprah's Lifeclass*. "And your real job in life is to figure out as soon as possible what that is, who you were meant to be, and to begin to honor that in the best way possible for yourself." ■

Who redefined the role of the First Lady?

Eleanor Roosevelt was the wife of the nation's 32nd president, Franklin D. Roosevelt, and the niece of President Theodore Roosevelt. She was also a leader in her own right. The First Lady was active in many political and social arenas. Today, she's remembered for her tireless efforts as a champion for the rights of women, minorities, and the poor. Her activism forever transformed the role of First Lady.

Roosevelt was born on October 11, 1884, in New York City. Though she was a shy and quiet child, her work on behalf of others led her to become a symbol of women's independence. Her interest in politics grew after her 1905 marriage to Franklin D. Roosevelt, a rising political star.

In 1921, he became stricken with polio. The illness paralyzed him from the waist down. Roosevelt increased her involvement in politics after this, in part to be her husband's "eyes and ears." But she did so to further her own goals, too.

In 1933, Roosevelt took her growing passion for social issues to the White House. Before Roosevelt, the role of the First Lady was mainly as a hostess. But she quickly changed that. During Franklin D. Roosevelt's presidency, she traveled the country giving lectures. When World War II broke out, she went overseas to boost the morale of U.S. troops. She used her role as First Lady to fight poverty and prejudice.

Roosevelt continued her public service after Franklin D. Roosevelt's death, in 1945. She served as a U.S. delegate to the United Nations and helped write the Universal Declaration of Human Rights, which outlines rights that everyone in the world should have. The achievement was one of her proudest moments. She's remembered as the First Lady of the World. ■

Roosevelt hosts a special party to honor servicemen at the White House in 1942.

Who is the scientist best known for her work with chimpanzees?

Jane Goodall has been fascinated with animals for as long as she can remember.

Growing up in England, her favorite books were *Tarzan* and *The Story of Doctor Doolittle*. These stories inspired her to live among wild animals herself.

When she was 26 years old, Goodall was given the chance to do just that. World-famous anthropologist Louis S. B. Leakey asked her to study a group of chimpanzees in Tanzania. Not much was known about the animals at the time. Goodall leapt at the opportunity. Armed with a note pad and binoculars, she set off for Africa.

The chimpanzees were wary of Goodall's presence at first. But she made careful observations, watching her subjects from afar. After a while, she gained the trust of the animals and they allowed her to come closer. She would spend the next 25 years studying the primates in their natural habitat. What she learned about chimpanzees fascinated people around the world.

One of her most important discoveries occurred in 1960, when she saw two male chimps strip the leaves from twigs and use the twigs to fish termites out of a termite mound. Until then, humans were thought to be the only species that made and used tools. She also discovered that chimps are not primarily vegetarians, as was previously thought.

In 1965, Goodall helped start the Gombe Stream Research Center, in Africa, so other scientists could also observe chimps. After studying the animals for the first part of her career, Goodall shifted her focus to conservation efforts for all creatures. She started the Jane Goodall Institute in 1977 to carry out this mission. The Institute's Roots & Shoots program encourages kids to take action to make the world a better place. ■

Goodall studies chimpanzees in Tanzania in 2006.

Thorpe shares his athletic gear with his sons, Phil and Billy, in 1931.

Who is regarded as the greatest athlete of all time?

In 1950, the Associated Press named **Jim Thorpe** the greatest athlete of the first half of the 20th century. More than 60 years later, many people think he has held onto the title.

James Francis Thorpe was born on May 28, 1888, in a small cabin near Prague, Oklahoma. Thorpe's father, Hiram, was a farmer. He and his wife, Charlotte, were both of mixed European and Native-American descent. They gave their son the Native-American name Wa-Tho-Huk, which means bright path in the Sac and Fox language.

Thorpe was a natural at sports. Growing up, he competed in football, track, baseball, lacrosse, hockey, handball, tennis, boxing, and even ballroom dancing.

Thorpe gained international fame in 1912, when he traveled with the U.S. ▶

▶ Olympic team to compete in the Summer Games in Stockholm, Sweden. Thorpe participated in the pentathlon and decathlon, taking gold in both events and setting Olympic records that stood for decades. The International Olympic Committee took away his medals and records after discovering he had played professional baseball from 1909 to 1910, but restored both in 1982.

After the Olympics, Thorpe spent six seasons as an outfielder in major-league baseball. He also played and coached professional football. One of Thorpe's lasting legacies was as cofounder and president of the American Professional Football Association, now known as the National Football League. Thorpe was inducted into the Pro Football Hall of Fame in 1963. ■

Who was the celebrated civil-rights activist who wrote *I Know Why the Caged Bird Sings?*

Maya Angelou was an acclaimed writer, teacher, and activist. Born Marguerite Johnson on April 4, 1928, in St. Louis, Missouri, Angelou grew up during a time when racial segregation was accepted in America's southern states. Having suffered many hardships early in life, Angelou persevered to become one of the most successful African-American literary giants of the 20th century—and one of the world's most influential voices.

Angelou received many honors for her work. She began her career as a performer, studying acting and dance in California. In the 1950s, she performed in several off-Broadway stage productions. But it was her 1969 memoir, *I Know Why the Caged Bird Sings*, that shot her to international stardom. The book, which described Angelou's younger years, made history as the first nonfiction bestseller written by an African-American woman.

After the success of her book, Angelou's acclaim grew. Her books, screenplays, and poetry wowed audiences and critics. One of Angelou's most famous poems was written for President Bill Clinton's inauguration in January 1993. She recited the poem, titled "On the Pulse of Morning," during the inaugural ceremony. She later won a Grammy for the audio version of the poem.

Angelou died on May 28, 2014. But her powerful words will live forever. ■

Who was the first American to orbit the Earth?

Before Neil Armstrong and Buzz Aldrin could even imagine walking on the moon, someone had to orbit the Earth. That someone was **John Glenn**.

The year was 1962, and the U.S. and the Soviet Union were in the midst of the great Space Race. The Soviets had sent cosmonaut Yuri Gagarin into orbit a year before. He was the first person in space. And while Alan Shepard and Gus Grissom soon became the first Americans in space, NASA had yet to send an astronaut into orbit. The U.S. space agency chose John Glenn to carry out the historic mission.

Glenn joined NASA after serving in the U.S. military. An experienced pilot, Glenn had ▶

● At age 77, Glenn prepares to soar into space aboard the space shuttle *Discovery*.

▶ flown dozens of combat missions during World War II and the Korean War. On February 20, 1962, Glenn rocketed into space aboard the Mercury capsule *Friendship 7*, becoming the first American to orbit the planet. During the nearly five-hour trip, Glenn circled the globe three times. The craft soared 162 miles above Earth at speeds as high as 17,500 miles per hour. The mission ended with Glenn splashing down safely in the Atlantic Ocean.

After his famed flight, President John F. Kennedy

Glenn goes for a drive with President Kennedy, who encouraged him to go into politics.

awarded Glenn the NASA Distinguished Service Medal. In 1974, Glenn was elected to the U.S. Senate. He served four terms in Congress as a Democrat from Ohio.

NASA came calling again in 1998. On October 29, 77-year-old Glenn launched into space again, aboard the space shuttle *Discovery*. The nine-day mission included an investigation of aging and space travel.

For his many contributions to space exploration and to his country, Glenn was awarded the Presidential Medal of Freedom by President Barack Obama in 2012. NASA has made much progress since Glenn first orbited the Earth, but he remains a symbol of American space exploration. ■

You Should Also Know ...

Sally Ride, first American woman in space

• Sally Ride always loved science and dreamed of exploring space. That wish came true on June 18, 1983, when she became the first American woman to travel into space.

Ride studied physics in college and in graduate school. She beat out 1,000 other applicants to be accepted into NASA's astronaut program. After intense training, she launched into history aboard the space shuttle *Challenger*.

Ride went into space again the following year, serving as a mission specialist for a second time. After retiring from NASA, she dedicated much of her time to inspiring kids—young girls especially—to get excited about science, technology, engineering, and math.

Who was a leading champion for people with disabilities?

With the help of her teacher Anne Sullivan (right), Keller learned new ways to communicate.

Helen Keller was born a happy and healthy baby on June 27, 1880, in Tuscumbia, Alabama. She began speaking at 6 months old, and walking at age 1. But tragedy struck when Keller was just 19 months old and an illness left her deaf and blind.

As she grew up, Keller found a way to communicate with the young daughter of the family's cook. But she also developed a wild streak, often throwing tantrums when she was unhappy.

In an attempt to help their daughter, Arthur and Katherine Keller sought the assistance of Alexander Graham Bell, the inventor of the telephone, who was working with deaf children. He suggested they visit the Perkins Institute for the Blind, in Boston, Massachusetts. There, they met the person who would change their daughter's life forever: Anne Sullivan.

Sullivan began helping the Kellers when Helen was only 6 years old. She didn't waste time getting to work. The 20-year-old taught her young student how to communicate by first having her touch an object, such as a doll. Then Sullivan would use sign language to spell out the name of the object in the palm of Keller's hand. The method worked, and within months, Keller began to communicate. Eventually, with Sullivan by her side, she was able to attend school. She graduated from college with honors in 1904.

During her lifetime, Keller fought for many causes, including equal rights for women. But she made it her life's core mission to improve the lives of people living with disabilities. She traveled the country giving lectures and shared her experiences in magazine articles and books. Keller also started Helen Keller International to help blind people in poor countries. She met 12 U.S. presidents through her activism. The Pulitzer Prize–winning play *The Miracle Worker* was based on her 1903 memoir, *The Story of My Life*.

Keller's life, work, and legacy prove that disabilities do not stand in the way of determination. ■

Who broke major-league baseball's color barrier?

On April 15, 1947, **Jackie Robinson** put on his Brooklyn Dodgers uniform and stepped onto Ebbets Field. He wasn't sure how the crowd would receive him, but he was ready to play ball.

Robinson was the first black player in major-league baseball. Until then, professional baseball had been racially segregated. These "color lines" had existed since the late 1800s. But Robinson broke through that color barrier when he signed with the Dodgers.

After Robinson played in his first major-league game, he received hate mail and death threats from prejudiced people. But he didn't let that stop him. He stepped up to the plate and became a legend.

In his first year with the Dodgers, Robinson stole a league-leading 29 bases and helped his team win the National League pennant. He was named MLB's first-ever Rookie of the Year. In 1949, he earned the National League Most Valuable Player award. And in 1955, he led the Dodgers to a World Series victory.

By the time he retired, in 1957, Robinson was an American hero, admired for both his strength of character and his baseball talent. He spent years fighting for civil rights, and his success opened doors for future black baseball players. In 1962, Robinson was the first African American inducted into the Baseball Hall of Fame. ■

Who led the movement for women's rights in the 1960s and 1970s?

Throughout the 1960s and 1970s, women fought to gain the same rights and respect as men. **Gloria Steinem** was on the front lines of that battle.

Fighting for gender equality runs in Steinem's family. Her grandmother was president of the Ohio Women's Suffrage Association from 1908 to 1911. The group fought for women's right to vote. While at Smith College in the 1950s, Steinem studied government, which wasn't a traditional major for women at the time. After graduating, she decided to become a writer.

Her activism grew partly from her work in journalism. Many of Steinem's articles looked at issues of inequality. In 1971, she teamed up with other respected feminists to start the National Women's Political Caucus, which encouraged women's participation in government.

The following year, she helped launch *Ms.* magazine, which explored women's issues. If you have you ever participated in "Take Our Daughters and Sons to Work Day," you can thank Steinem for helping to create that program, too.

It's been decades since Steinem became a leader of the women's movement, but she continues to advocate for gender equality.

"I never wanted to be a politician or elected person myself, so I loved to work for other women who did—and hope that more girls will do that," Steinem told *Teen Vogue* in 2011. ■

Leaders and

Changemakers

Who became the first African-American president of the U.S.?

On January 20, 2009, **Barack Obama** was sworn in as the 44th president of the United States, becoming the first African American to be elected to the nation's highest office. He was reelected in 2012.

Barack Obama II was born on August 4, 1961, in Hawaii. The name *Barack* comes from the Arabic and Swahili words meaning "blessed." Obama's parents were students at the University of Hawaii at Manoa when they met. His father, Barack Obama Sr., was from Nyanza Province, in Kenya. His mother, Ann Dunham, was from Wichita, Kansas.

When Obama was 2 years old, his parents separated. His father eventually moved back to Kenya. His mother later married Lolo Soetoro, a University of Hawaii student from Indonesia, and the family moved to Jakarta, Indonesia. There, Obama's half-sister, Maya, was born. Barry, as his friends and family called him, lived in

Indonesia for four years.

At age 10, he moved back to the U.S. to live with his maternal grandparents, Stanley and Madelyn Dunham, in Hawaii. He attended Punahou, a prep school. He filled his days body surfing, singing in the choir, spending time with friends, and developing a love of basketball—he still plays in regular pick-up games today.

Obama went to Occidental College, in Los Angeles, California. He later transferred to Columbia University, in New York City. During his college years, Obama started going by his full name, Barack.

Obama earned his law degree from Harvard University and went on to become a civil-rights lawyer and law professor. He met his future wife, Michelle Robinson, in Chicago, Illinois. They married in 1992 and had two daughters, Malia and Sasha.

Obama served as an Illinois state senator for eight years. In 2004, he was elected to the U.S. Senate. At the 2004 Democratic National Convention, Obama gave a powerful speech that helped him gain enough recognition to begin vying for the 2008 Democratic presidential nomination.

As president, Obama has made it his mission to improve health care, restore the economy, change immigration policies, protect the environment, and promote world peace. His policies have faced much opposition, but Obama continues to forge ahead in an effort to fulfill his promises to the American people and to leave a lasting legacy. ■

Who led India's fight for independence from Britain?

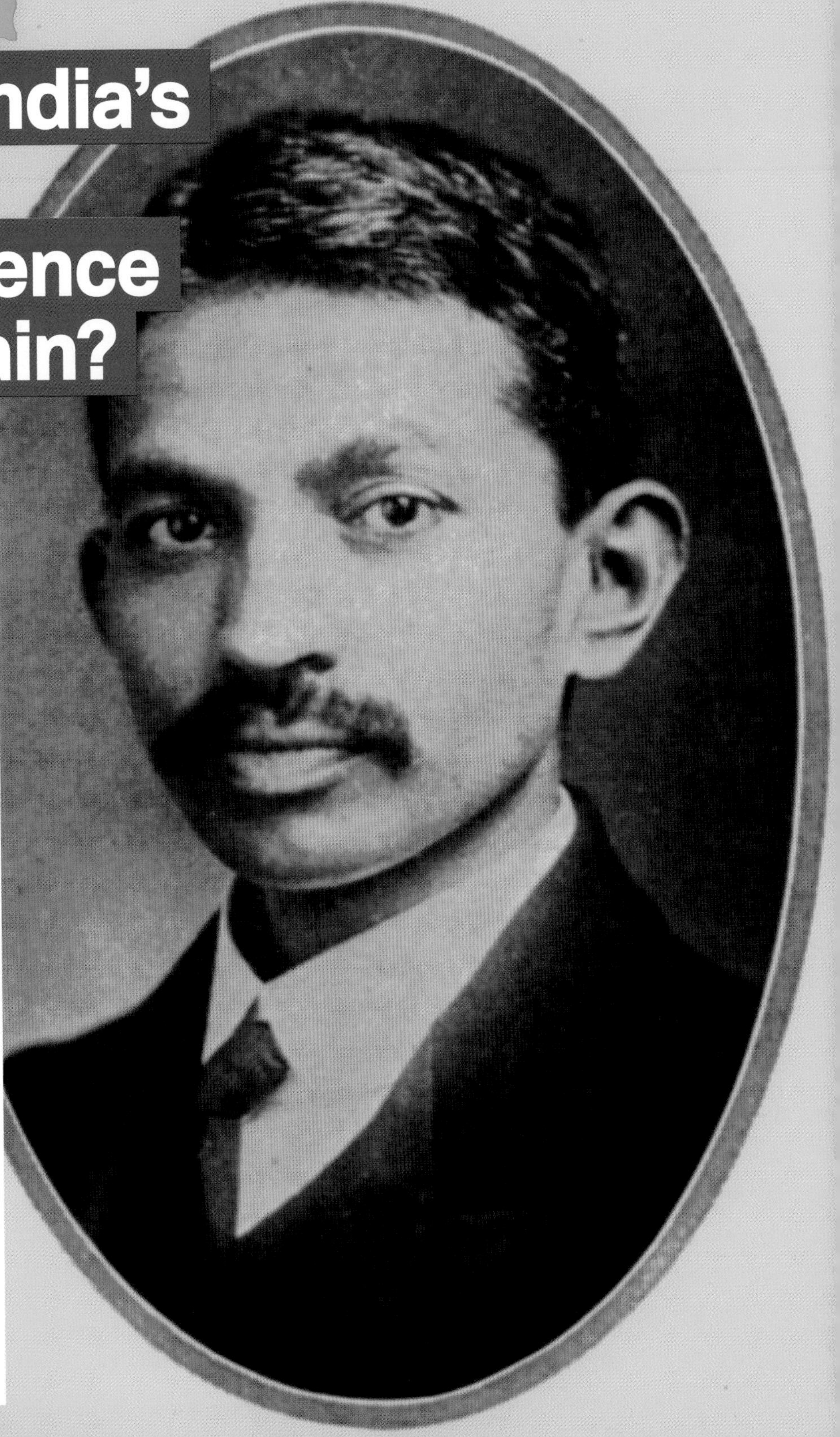

Mohandas Gandhi believed in equality and religious freedom for all. Known as Mahatma, or "great soul," Gandhi led India in its struggle to win independence from British rule. The spiritual man encouraged his millions of followers to use peaceful forms of protest to achieve their goals. "An eye for an eye only ends up making the whole world blind," he wisely once said. Gandhi's leadership changed India's history and inspired other civil-rights movements around the world.

Gandhi was born on October 2, 1869, in Porbandar, Gujarat, in northwestern India. He moved to London, England, to study law at age 18 and later accepted a job at an Indian law firm in South Africa. While working there, he saw the racial bias experienced by Indian immigrants and the prejudice he faced personally. He decided to do something about it.

It was around this time that Gandhi developed his famous philosophy of nonviolent protest. He spent more than 20 years in South Africa fighting for equal rights for his countrymen. When he returned to India in 1914, he joined the struggle for Indian independence. He went to jail for civil disobedience several times and went on a hunger strike for 21 days. One of his most famous protests was the Salt March. After Britain put a tax on salt, Gandhi organized a 240-mile walk to the sea to collect salt as a symbol of opposition. Thousands of people marched with him.

Britain finally granted India independence in 1947. Gandhi then turned his attention to ending the fighting between Hindus and Muslims in the region. He was assassinated in 1948, but his teachings and dedication to peace and justice endure to this day. ■

Who was the first Polish cardinal to be elected pope?

After centuries of Italian popes, the election of **Karol Józef Wojtyla** (voy-*tee*-wah) as the new leader of the Catholic Church surprised the world. In 1978, Wojtyla, the archbishop of Krakow, became the first pope to come from Poland. Known as John Paul II, he spent 27 years as pontiff, making him one of the longest-serving popes in modern history.

Wojtyla was born on May 18, 1920, in Wadowice, Poland. As a young man, he experienced the struggles of living under Nazi rule when Germany occupied Poland during World War II.

Being deeply religious, Wojtyla wanted to join the priesthood. But the Nazis didn't believe in higher education for non-Germans and didn't allow them access to universities, including seminaries, which are schools that train students to become ministers or priests. Wojtyla studied in secret at an underground seminary in Krakow. He was ordained in 1946 and rose through the ranks to become a cardinal.

When Wojtyla was elected as pope in 1978, he took the name John Paul II. As leader of the Catholic Church, Pope John Paul II traveled the world spreading the message of faith and peace. He sought to repair divisions within the church and to strengthen the relationship between the Catholic Church and other religions. John Paul II was also a vocal human-rights advocate. His humility, dignity, and strength earned him the respect of most people he met. But in 1981, an assassin tried to kill him. The gunshot left him seriously injured, but alive. He went on to make a full recovery. John Paul II died on April 2, 2005, at age 84. More than 3 million people came to St. Peter's Basilica, in Vatican City, to pay their respects before his funeral. Nine years after his death, the Catholic Church declared John Paul II a saint. ■

Who was the youngest person to receive the Nobel Peace Prize?

Malala Yousafzai was 17 years old when she was awarded the 2014 Nobel Peace Prize, becoming the youngest winner in history.

A youth activist from Pakistan, Malala began fighting for girls' right to education when she was only 11 years old. She wrote a blog about the Taliban's takeover of her hometown of Mingora, in northwestern Pakistan. The Taliban follow an extreme version of Islam. They believe girls should not go to school.

For months, Malala's school and hundreds of others in the district of Swat were closed. Malala spoke out publicly and began to blog about her desire to go to school. "All I want is an education," she said in an interview.

When the Pakistani government regained control of the region, Malala returned to class. But she continued to speak out about equal rights to education. On October 9, 2012, the Taliban tried to silence her. A gunman boarded her school bus and shot her on the left side of her forehead. Malala survived. Ever courageous, she didn't let the Taliban stop her. She became a symbol of the struggle for girls' rights all over the world.

Now she's also a worldwide symbol of courage and peace. Nine months after she was shot, she gave a speech at the United Nations. "They thought that the bullets would silence us. But they failed," she said. "And then, out of that silence came thousands of voices ... Weakness, fear, and hopelessness died. Strength, power, and courage [were] born." ■

Who was South Africa's first black president?

● Mandela greets supporters at a rally one month before his election in 1994.

Nelson Mandela's commitment to his country changed South Africa from a nation torn apart by racism to a country on the path to peace. After spending close to three decades in prison for fighting against racial injustice, he went on to make history as South Africa's first democratically elected president.

Mandela was born Rolihlahla Mandela on July 18, 1918, in a small South African village. As a young boy, he was sent to live with a local tribal chief. While in school, Mandela learned all about his ancestors' struggles with discrimination. He wanted to help his countrymen. Eventually, he moved to Johannesburg to study law, and later opened the country's first black law practice. He also joined the African National Congress, a group that fought for racial equality.

The South African government introduced a policy called apartheid in 1948. The system separated people of different races in all aspects of life. People who were not white had few choices and even less opportunity. Mandela traveled the country, encouraging people to take part in nonviolent protests against the discriminatory policies. He was sent to prison for his beliefs, but he kept battling for equality, even from his cell. People everywhere protested Mandela's imprisonment.

"I have cherished the ideal of a democratic and free society in which all persons live together in harmony and with ▶

Mandela attends a victory march for his political party, the African National Congress, in 1994.

equal opportunities," he said during his trial. "It is an ideal for which I hope to live for and to see realized. But if needs be, it is an ideal for which I am prepared to die."

Mandela spent 27 years in prison, until February 11, 1990, when South African president F.W. de Klerk released him. The two worked together to end apartheid, and won the Nobel Peace Prize for their efforts in 1993.

In 1994, nonwhites were finally granted the right to vote in South Africa. Mandela became the nation's first democratically elected president, and the country's first black president. During his time in office, he worked to improve housing, education, and economic opportunities for the country's large black population.

Mandela left office in 1999,

but continued his mission to spread peace around the globe. In 2007, he helped found The Elders, a group of world leaders committed to ending conflicts and promoting human rights. Mandela died following a long illness in 2013. He was 95 years old. ■

You Should Also Know ...

Desmond Tutu, South African activist

• As a young boy growing up in South Africa, Desmond Tutu knew he was being treated unfairly because of the color of his skin. Despite the racism, he resolved to keep a positive outlook on life.

In 1975, Tutu became the first black African to be appointed the dean of St. Mary's Cathedral in Johannesburg. Eventually, he was elected the first black archbishop of Cape Town. He used the spotlight to speak out against apartheid, calling for equal rights for all South Africans.

His efforts caught the attention of the world. In 1984, he received the Nobel Peace Prize. Other countries soon started to put pressure on the South African government to end the discrimination. The work of leaders like Tutu and Nelson Mandela led to the end of apartheid in 1994.

Who was the oldest elected U.S. president?

Ronald Reagan was 69 years old when he took office on January 20, 1981, making him the oldest person in history to win the presidency. As the 40th president of the U.S., he was best known for leading the nation during the end of the Cold War and for his economic policies at home. But he didn't always have political aspirations. As a Hollywood movie star, Reagan never imagined a life in politics. He appeared in more than 50 films and had a full career as an actor. His political interests led him to run for governor of California, and his fame and charm helped him win. He won the race for governor in 1966 and was reelected in 1970. Ten years later, he won the 1980 Republican presidential nomination, and months later, the national election.

One of the defining events of Reagan's presidency was the end of the Cold War. Since World War II, the U.S. and the Soviet Union had been locked in an era of distrust. Both countries had nuclear bombs, and each side worried about what the other would do with the

● Reagan stars in the Western movie *Law and Order* in 1953.

powerful weapons.

Reagan was committed to building a stronger America and to winning the Cold War. But he also wanted to work toward peace. When Mikhail Gorbachev became the Soviet Union's leader in 1985, Reagan saw hope for U.S.–Soviet relations. After years of negotiations, the two leaders signed a historic agreement in 1987 for both countries to reduce nuclear arms.

Reagan is remembered for his ability to reach people with his words. He was a gifted speaker who could connect with everyone from world leaders to local farmers. This important skill earned him the nickname the Great Communicator and made him one of the most admired presidents of our time. ■

● King delivers his "I Have a Dream" speech to a crowd of about 250,000 at the March on Washington, in August 1963.

Whose leadership shaped the civil-rights movement?

"I have a dream that my four little children will one day live in a nation where they will not be judged by the color of their skin, but by the content of their character." **Martin Luther King Jr.** delivered these famous lines as part of his "I Have A Dream" speech on August 28, 1963, during the March on Washington for Jobs and Freedom. The event is remembered as one of the most important moments of the civil-rights movement of the 1950s and 1960s. It was held to peacefully protest racial discrimination and to demand the passage of civil-rights laws in Congress.

In the early 1960s, segregation, or the separation of people by race, was accepted in many parts of the U.S., particularly in the South. Black people and white people ▶

King and his wife, Coretta Scott King, watch their children Martin Luther III and Yolanda play at home in 1960.

could not attend the same schools, sit next to each other on buses, or even use the same water fountains.

As a leader of the civil-rights movement, King fought to change this unfair treatment. King was a Baptist minister and an activist. He believed in achieving justice through nonviolence. His leadership played a critical role in ending racial segregation in America, and in the passing of the Civil Rights Act of 1964 and the Voting Rights Act of 1965. For his tireless efforts to improve race relations in America, King received the Nobel Peace Prize in 1964.

King was assassinated

on April 4, 1968, before he could see his dream fully realized. Each year around his birthday, a day of service in his honor celebrates his vision, courage, and leadership. ■

You Should Also Know ...

Yuri Kochiyama, civil-rights leader

• Japanese American Yuri Kochiyama was a lifelong champion of equal rights. Born Mary Yuriko Nakahara on May 19, 1921, Kochiyama and her family—along with tens of thousands of other Americans of Japanese descent—were forced into internment camps during World War II. This unjust treatment lit a spark in her, leading her to dedicate her life to fighting for civil rights for people of many races.

While at the camp, she met her future husband, William Kochiyama, a soldier in the 442nd Regimental Combat Team, a courageous group of Japanese-American troops. After the war, the couple became more involved in the civil-rights movement.

In 1963, Kochiyama met controversial civil-rights leader Malcolm X, who encouraged African Americans to fight for equality "by any means necessary." While Kochiyama initially disagreed with some of his viewpoints, the two became fast friends. Kochiyama remained a steadfast advocate for civil rights until her death in 2014. Her activism led the U.S. Senate to formally apologize to Japanese Americans in 1988.

Whose foundation gives nearly $4 billion to charity each year?

Bill Gates made his name as the billionaire co-founder of software giant Microsoft. But his charity work also defines him. Bill and his wife, **Melinda**, run the Bill & Melinda Gates Foundation, which provides funding to groups that tackle world issues involving health, hunger, poverty, and education. They created the foundation to use their wealth to contribute to the common good.

Between 2000 and 2014, the foundation gave away more than $30 billion dollars in global aid. The Gates Foundation has made it a top priority to combat infectious diseases, such as polio, Ebola, and AIDS, in poor countries.

The organization is best known for its commitment to stamping out malaria, which affects more than 200 million people in nearly 100 countries. The disease is transmitted by infected mosquitos and can spread quickly. Hundreds of thousands of people die from malaria every year, mostly in Sub-Saharan Africa.

Malaria can be prevented and treated. That's where Bill and Melinda Gates have stepped in. Their foundation partners with organizations to deliver insecticide-treated bed nets, medicines, and other important tools. They are also working to develop lifesaving vaccines. With enough resources, malaria can potentially be eliminated for good.

"I believe it's not only possible to eradicate malaria; I believe it's necessary," Bill Gates wrote of the foundation's goal. "Ultimately, the cost of controlling it endlessly is not sustainable. The only way to stop this disease is to end it forever." ■

Who led Britain to victory during World War II?

The nickname British Bulldog suited the gruff and staunch **Winston Churchill**. Many consider the former British prime minister to be one of the greatest leaders of the 20th century, largely due to his unshakable leadership during World War II. Even after France and other countries in Western Europe had fallen to Nazi Germany, Churchill urged his countrymen to fight on.

Churchill's rousing speeches gave Britain the resolve to stand strong. In Churchill's first speech to Parliament after becoming prime minister, he said of the war: "You ask, what is our aim? I can answer in one word: It is victory, victory at all costs, victory in spite of all terror, victory, however long and hard the road may be; for without victory, there is no survival." Britain's persistence, together with the other Allied forces, led to the defeat of the Nazis.

Churchill came from a long line of politicians and statesmen. In 1900, he was elected to Parliament. He held a number of different positions in the British government over the next three decades. On May 10, 1940, King George VI appointed Churchill to be Britain's prime minister.

Despite his celebrated wartime leadership, Churchill lost the 1945 election for prime minister. But he was elected to office again in 1951. Though health problems forced him to retire as prime minister in 1955, Churchill remained an active member of Parliament almost until his death, at age 90, in 1965. ■

Who was the U.S. president who negotiated an end to the Cuban Missile Crisis?

President **John F. Kennedy** faced many challenges during his short time in office. But no issue proved as urgent as the Cuban Missile Crisis of October 1962.

The crisis began when the Soviet Union started secretly building nuclear missile bases in Cuba, an island country 110 miles off the coast of Florida. If installed, these missiles could have struck any point in the U.S. This threat caused great concern for Americans.

At the time of the conflict, relations between the United States and the Soviet Union were already rocky. Since the end of World War II, the two superpowers had been locked in a long period of distrust. This era was known as the Cold War. Because of this distrust, both countries had spent money building nuclear weapons. But when the U.S. learned of the Soviet plan to put missiles in such close range, Kennedy issued a stern warning: He wasn't going to let it happen.

For 13 intense days of negotiations, the nations prepared for a possible war. Finally, Soviet leaders agreed to remove the missiles from Cuba and the U.S. agreed not to invade the island nation. The U.S. also agreed to remove its own missiles from Turkey. Nuclear war had been avoided. The event strengthened Kennedy's image both at home and abroad, and set the tone for the rest of his time in office.

The Democratic Party had nominated Kennedy to be its candidate for president in 1960. He asked Lyndon B. Johnson, a senator from Texas, to run with him as vice president. On November 8, 1960, Kennedy narrowly defeated Richard Nixon to become the 35th president of the U.S.

At 43 years old, Kennedy was the youngest president ever elected to office. He was also the nation's first Roman Catholic president. During his inaugural speech, he called for his fellow Americans to be more active as citizens. "Ask not what your country can do for you, ask what you can do for your country," he said.

As president, Kennedy pushed Congress to approve funding for space exploration, created the Peace Corps, and championed civil-rights reform. One of his final acts as head of state was to introduce a new civil-rights bill into Congress. The bill would later be signed into law as the Civil Rights Act of 1964. But Kennedy would not live to see it happen.

On November 21, 1963,

President Kennedy flew to Texas with his wife, Jacqueline. He was scheduled to give several speeches while campaigning for reelection. The next day, the couple greeted cheering crowds while riding through downtown Dallas in a convertible. Gun shots rang out. A 24-year-old warehouse worker named Lee Harvey Oswald had fired at the car, hitting the president twice. Kennedy was rushed to the hospital, where he later died. Police arrested Oswald within hours of the shooting.

The nation and the world mourned the fallen leader. He was 46 years old. Hundreds of thousands of people gathered in Washington, D.C., for his funeral. Millions watched the service on television. Though his time was cut short, he is remembered as one of America's most popular presidents. ■

Who was Israel's first female prime minister?

Golda Meir served as Israel's first woman prime minister from 1969 to 1974. She was only the third female prime minister in the world. Often called the Iron Lady of Israel, Meir was known for her strong will, honest and straightforward manner, and passion for politics.

Meir was born in Kiev, Ukraine, in 1898. She grew up in Milwaukee, Wisconsin. As a teenager, she developed a passionate interest in creating a Jewish state. She was among the signers of the Israeli Declaration of Independence on May 14, 1948, when the State of Israel was established. She served in several roles in Israel's government before becoming prime minister in 1969.

Meir focused her term on diplomacy. She pushed for a peace settlement with the Arab states, which had been at war with Israel since the country gained statehood. During Meir's time as prime minister, the region enjoyed a three-year cease-fire. But that ended in October 1973 with the Yom Kippur War.

On a Jewish holy day, Egypt and Syria attacked territories occupied by Israel. Israeli forces suffered heavy losses, but eventually were able to push back.

Meir received much criticism for Israel's lack of preparedness for the war. She resigned from office in 1974, but remained an important political figure until her death in 1978. ■

Who won the Nobel Peace Prize for her charity work in India?

Mother Teresa devoted her life to helping the poor, the sick, and the needy in India. Mother Teresa was born Agnes Gonxha Bojaxhiu (*Ag*-ness Gohn-*jah* Boh-*yah*-joo) in what is now Skopje, Macedonia, in 1910. Having grown up in a deeply religious Roman Catholic family, she felt called to serve the church at a young age. At 18, she left home for a nunnery in Ireland. There, she took the name Sister Mary Teresa. When she finished her studies in 1929, she was sent to Calcutta, India, to teach at St. Mary's School for girls.

In 1937, Sister Mary Teresa took her final vows, becoming Mother Teresa. As the principal at St. Mary's, she was known for her kindness and generosity.

On September 10, 1946, Mother Teresa was on a train from Calcutta to Darjeeling when she felt a second calling—"a call within a call"—to help the needy while living among them. She worked in the slums of Calcutta, where she founded a new sisterhood, the Missionaries of Charity. Her organization cared for the sick and needy. Mother Teresa also became an Indian citizen. She expanded her work to other parts of the country and, eventually, had foundations around the entire world.

Mother Teresa's charity work earned her the 1979 Nobel Peace Prize and the Presidential Medal of Freedom. After she died on September 5, 1997, she was given a state funeral by the government of India. ■

Who said, "Speak softly and carry a big stick"?

In explaining how to handle political opponents, **Theodore Roosevelt** famously quoted the African proverb, "Speak softly and carry a big stick; you will go far." The 26th president of the U.S. believed in striving for peace, while also establishing the power of the U.S. military. This policy was known as big-stick diplomacy.

Roosevelt championed the construction of the Panama Canal, which connects the Atlantic and Pacific Oceans. A canal is a man-made waterway built to allow the passage of boats. There was a great need for a shortcut between the Atlantic and Pacific Oceans. At the time, Panama was part of Colombia, which rejected the U.S. plan to build the canal. In response, Roosevelt sent warships to Panama City in

Roosevelt, pictured above in Yosemite Valley, California, in 1903, is one of four presidents to be immortalized on Mount Rushmore (right).

support of a revolution that would lead to Panama's independence, in 1903. The new government allowed the U.S. to build the critical canal. In 1906, Roosevelt visited the canal's construction site. This trip made him the first American president to leave the country while in office. The canal was successfully completed in 1914.

When Roosevelt took office in 1901, he was only 42 years old—the youngest president in the nation's history at that time. Roosevelt, a war hero and the former governor of New York, was vice president when President William McKinley was assassinated, less than a year into his second term. Roosevelt was sworn in as president. In this role, he achieved as much domestically as he did abroad. One of his lasting legacies was in environmental conservation. In 1906, Roosevelt signed the Antiquities Act, which protected historic and natural sites, including Arizona's Grand Canyon and California's Muir Woods. It also allowed the president or Congress to establish national monuments. The progressive president also supported desegregation and equal voting rights for women. ■

Whose book launched the modern environmental movement?

Rachel Carson changed the world when she wrote *Silent Spring*. The best-selling book warned of the dangers of misusing chemical pesticides and their harmful effects on humans, animals, lakes, and oceans. Its release in 1962 helped spur the modern-day environmental movement.

Carson was born May 27, 1907, on a farm in Springdale, Pennsylvania. Her mother encouraged her enthusiasm for learning about the natural world, and for writing.

Carson became a marine biologist and worked for the U.S. Fish and Wildlife Service from 1936 to 1952. She wrote several articles and books about the importance of protecting the environment, but *Silent Spring* made the biggest impact. Carson hoped her book would help people understand that toxins that enter the ground (in particular the pesticide DDT) go on to enter the food chain, which can sicken people, animals, and the environment.

President John F. Kennedy ordered the Science Advisory Committee to look at the issue. Carson's trailblazing efforts launched an ongoing green revolution that continues today. ■

Who was the British prime minister known as the Iron Lady?

Margaret Thatcher was Britain's first female prime minister. Thatcher held the position from 1979 until 1990, making her the only person to serve three consecutive terms as Britain's top elected official. While in office, Thatcher transformed the nation's economy and politics. Her high standards and strong will earned her the nickname Britain's Iron Lady.

Thatcher studied chemistry at Oxford University, but her real passion was politics. In 1959, she won her first elected position as the Member of Parliament from Finchley, an area of North London. In 1970, Thatcher was named the secretary of state for education and science. In 1975, she was elected leader of the Conservative Party, making her the first woman to lead a major political party in Britain. Then, in 1979, she became prime minister.

Thatcher was a conservative leader who believed in limiting the government's power. She worked to cut public expenses and income taxes, and fought against labor unions. Her tough political style made her unpopular in Britain. But her swift handling of a conflict over the British territory of the Falkland Islands, off the coast of Argentina, restored the British people's faith in Thatcher, who was reelected in 1983 and in 1987. Though Thatcher was forced to resign in 1990, she stayed in Parliament until she retired in 1992. ■

Whose refusal to change seats changed the nation?

December 1, 1955, began like any other day for **Rosa Parks**. But business as usual soon transformed into a crucial turning point in U.S. history, and turned the department-store seamstress into a central figure of the civil-rights movement. On that historic day, Parks broke the law. Her crime? Refusing to give up her seat on a public bus in Montgomery, Alabama. This quiet but powerful act spurred the Montgomery Bus Boycott—and changed our nation's history.

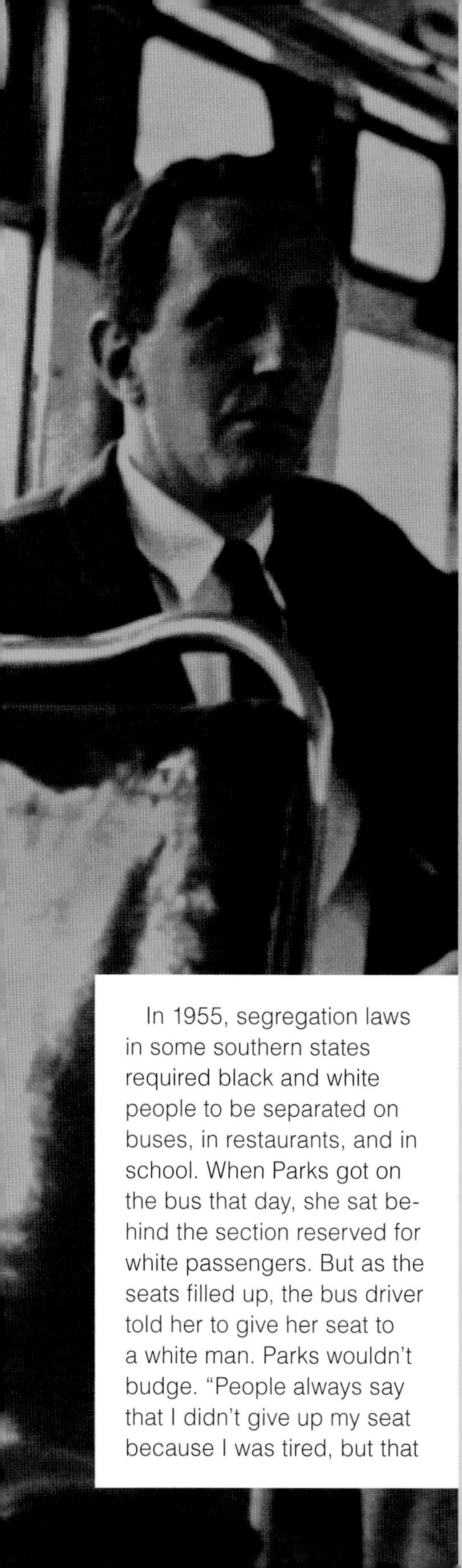

In 1955, segregation laws in some southern states required black and white people to be separated on buses, in restaurants, and in school. When Parks got on the bus that day, she sat behind the section reserved for white passengers. But as the seats filled up, the bus driver told her to give her seat to a white man. Parks wouldn't budge. "People always say that I didn't give up my seat because I was tired, but that isn't true," she said. "The only tired I was, was tired of giving in."

Parks was arrested that day, but her courage inspired others. African Americans responded to the injustice by refusing to ride the buses in Montgomery. During that time, about three-quarters of bus riders in the city were black. Martin Luther King Jr. led the peaceful boycott.

After 381 days, the U.S. Supreme Court ruled that African Americans could not be forced to sit in certain areas on buses. In 1964, Congress passed the Civil Rights Act, which outlawed segregation in all public places.

Parks received many honors in her lifetime, including the Presidential Medal of Freedom. The civil-rights pioneer died on October 24, 2005. She was 92 years old. She'll forever be remembered as the leader who took a stand by taking a seat. ■

Who was the only U.S. president to serve four terms in office?

Roosevelt (front row, center) joins members of the U.S. military aboard the cruiser *Indianapolis* in 1934.

Franklin D. Roosevelt is the only U.S. president to serve more than two terms in the White House. While in office, from 1932 to 1945, he led America through the Great Depression and World War II. Despite facing many challenges as president, Roosevelt forged ahead, inspiring hope and confidence in the American people.

Franklin Delano Roosevelt was born on January 30, 1882, in Hyde Park, New York. Roosevelt attended Harvard University and went on to study law at Columbia University. He worked as a lawyer for three years at a prestigious New York City law firm before entering politics in 1910, when he was elected to the New York State Senate as a Democrat for his home district. He was reelected in 1912.

In 1913, President Woodrow Wilson made Roosevelt the assistant secretary of the Navy. Roosevelt held the

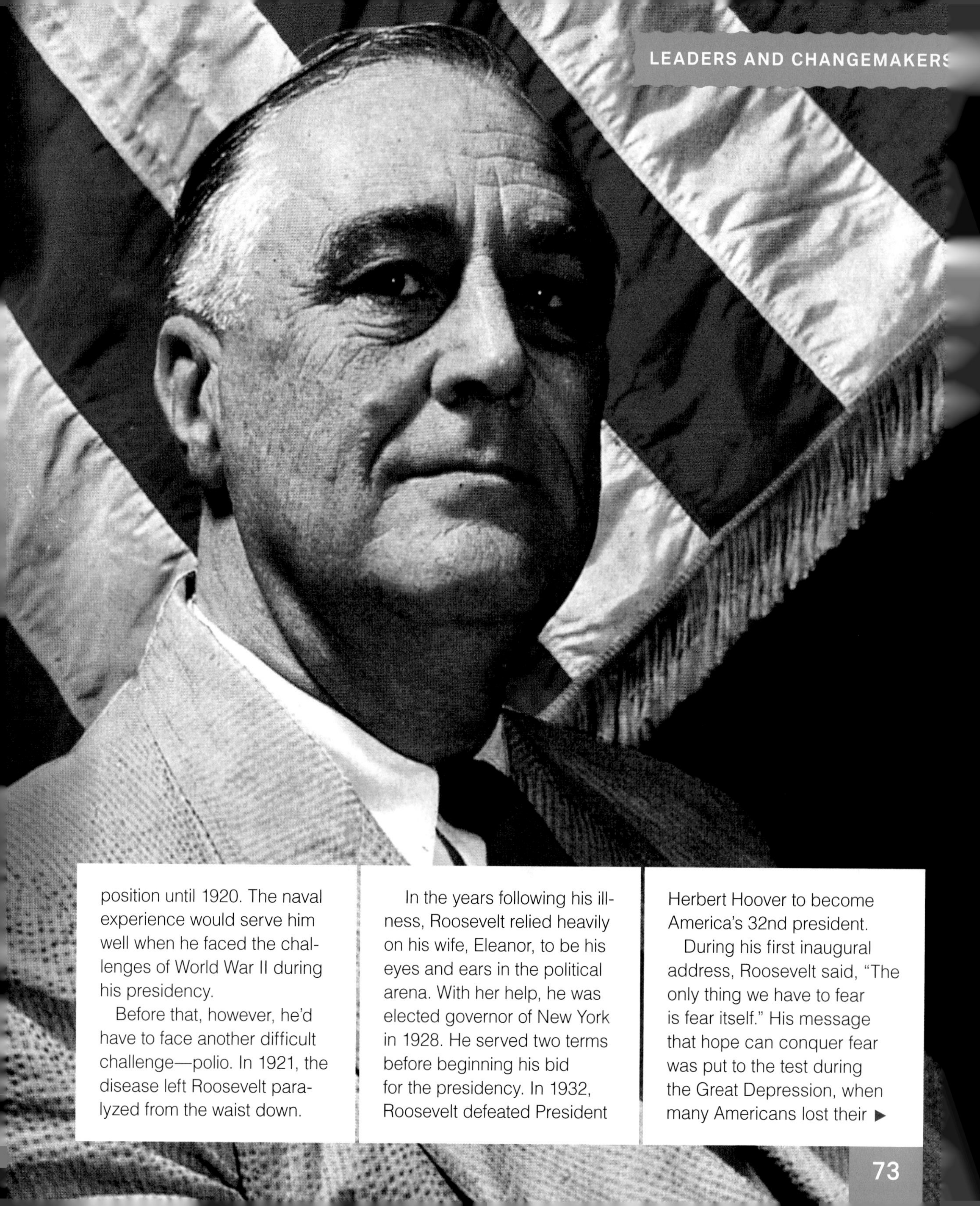

position until 1920. The naval experience would serve him well when he faced the challenges of World War II during his presidency.

Before that, however, he'd have to face another difficult challenge—polio. In 1921, the disease left Roosevelt paralyzed from the waist down.

In the years following his illness, Roosevelt relied heavily on his wife, Eleanor, to be his eyes and ears in the political arena. With her help, he was elected governor of New York in 1928. He served two terms before beginning his bid for the presidency. In 1932, Roosevelt defeated President Herbert Hoover to become America's 32nd president.

During his first inaugural address, Roosevelt said, "The only thing we have to fear is fear itself." His message that hope can conquer fear was put to the test during the Great Depression, when many Americans lost their ▶

▶ jobs and life savings. In Roosevelt's first 100 days as president, he introduced the New Deal, a government program to help the economy and the people. The New Deal included Social Security to help retired people, work programs, aid for farmers, and more. His radio addresses, or fireside chats, also helped Roosevelt earn the public's trust in his plans.

When World War II broke out in Europe, Roosevelt tried to keep America neutral, though he offered aid to Great Britain. But with the surprise attack by the Japanese on Hawaii's Pearl Harbor on December 7, 1941, Roosevelt knew the nation could no longer sit on the sidelines. The entry of the U.S. into World War II helped turn the tide of the war and led to victory for the Allied forces over the Axis Powers.

Roosevelt felt that future peace depended on keeping alliances between nations intact. To that end, he proposed the creation of a peacekeeping organization—the United Nations.

The stress of the war greatly affected Roosevelt's health. On April 12, 1945, he died from a stroke. He was 63. Roosevelt was still in office at the time, so Vice President Harry S. Truman took over the nation's top job. Following Roosevelt's death, Congress passed a law that allowed U.S. presidents to serve a maximum of two terms. ■

• Roosevelt signs a declaration of war on Germany and Italy in 1941.

You Should Also Know ...

Frances Perkins, champion of the working class

• President Franklin D. Roosevelt appointed Frances Perkins as his secretary of labor in 1933. She was the first woman to hold a cabinet position in the U.S., and served in the role for 12 years—longer than anyone else to date.

Perkins played a key part in drafting New Deal legislation, including minimum-wage laws. But one of her most important contributions was as chairwoman of the President's Committee on Economic Security. In this position, she helped shape the Social Security Act of 1935.

By the time she died, in 1965, Perkins was more than just the first woman cabinet member. In her lifetime, Perkins achieved a variety of important social reforms that still stand today. She was a champion for laborers everywhere.

Artists and

Entertainers

● One Direction celebrates the launch of their debut single, "What Makes You Beautiful," in London in 2011.

Who is the boy band that rose to fame on reality TV?

They came to *The X Factor,* Britain's televised singing competition, as five solo contestants in 2010. But they left as the boy-band sensation **One Direction**. Since appearing on the seventh season of the popular talent show, the members of the band have become international superstars. They ▶

1D thrills an audience in Las Vegas, Nevada, during the 2014 iHeartRadio Music Festival.

▶ have released multiple chart-topping albums and have played several sold-out world tours. They even conquered the box office with their concert documentary, *One Direction: This Is Us*, about their phenomenal rise to fame.

Singers Niall Horan, Zayn Malik, Harry Styles, Louis Tomlinson, and Liam Payne had been competing separately on *The X Factor*. Guest judge Nicole Scherzinger suggested that they perform together, so the boys joined forces to form One Direction. It turned out to be the best decision they ever made.

The group earned third place in the competition. But

their charm and vocal talent would soon go platinum. Judge Simon Cowell recognized their potential star power, and signed them to his record label.

One Direction—or 1D, as fans call the band—released their first single, "What Makes You Beautiful," in 2011. Their debut album, *Up All Night*, followed. With the album's release in the U.S., One Direction became the first British-Irish band to debut at the top of the Billboard 200 chart, selling more than 176,000 copies in its first week.

A year later, their second album, *Take Me Home*, included hit singles "Live While We're Young" and "Little Things." They wrote their third studio album, *Midnight Memories*, while on tour. That album, which hit Number 1 in seven countries, included "Best Song Ever" and the soulful "Story of My Life."

With their 2014 album, *Four*, the quintet scored their fourth Number 1 album in only three years. Not to mention they were named the top global recording artist of 2013. And while original member Malik left the band in March 2015, the remaining boys of 1D are still proving that the only direction they are headed is up. ■

You Should Also Know ...

The Beatles, legendary rockers

• Decades before the members of 1D were born, a British quartet called the Beatles revolutionized pop music. The 1960s rock 'n' roll band, which included John Lennon, Paul McCartney, George Harrison, and Ringo Starr, became one of the biggest musical acts of all time.

Known as the Fab Four, the shaggy-haired young men from Liverpool, England, had an innovative and modern sound that set them apart. They enjoyed great success in Britain and made their first American appearance on *The Ed Sullivan Show* in February 1964. More than 70 million people tuned in to see them perform their single "I Want to Hold Your Hand" and other hits, launching Beatlemania into full swing.

The band produced many chart-topping songs and sold more than 1 billion records. Their ability to reinvent themselves with every new album also kept audiences wanting more. Though the band broke up in 1970, timeless tracks like "Hey Jude," "Yesterday," and "Let It Be" continue to find new fans with every generation.

Who helped bring The Hunger Games to the big screen?

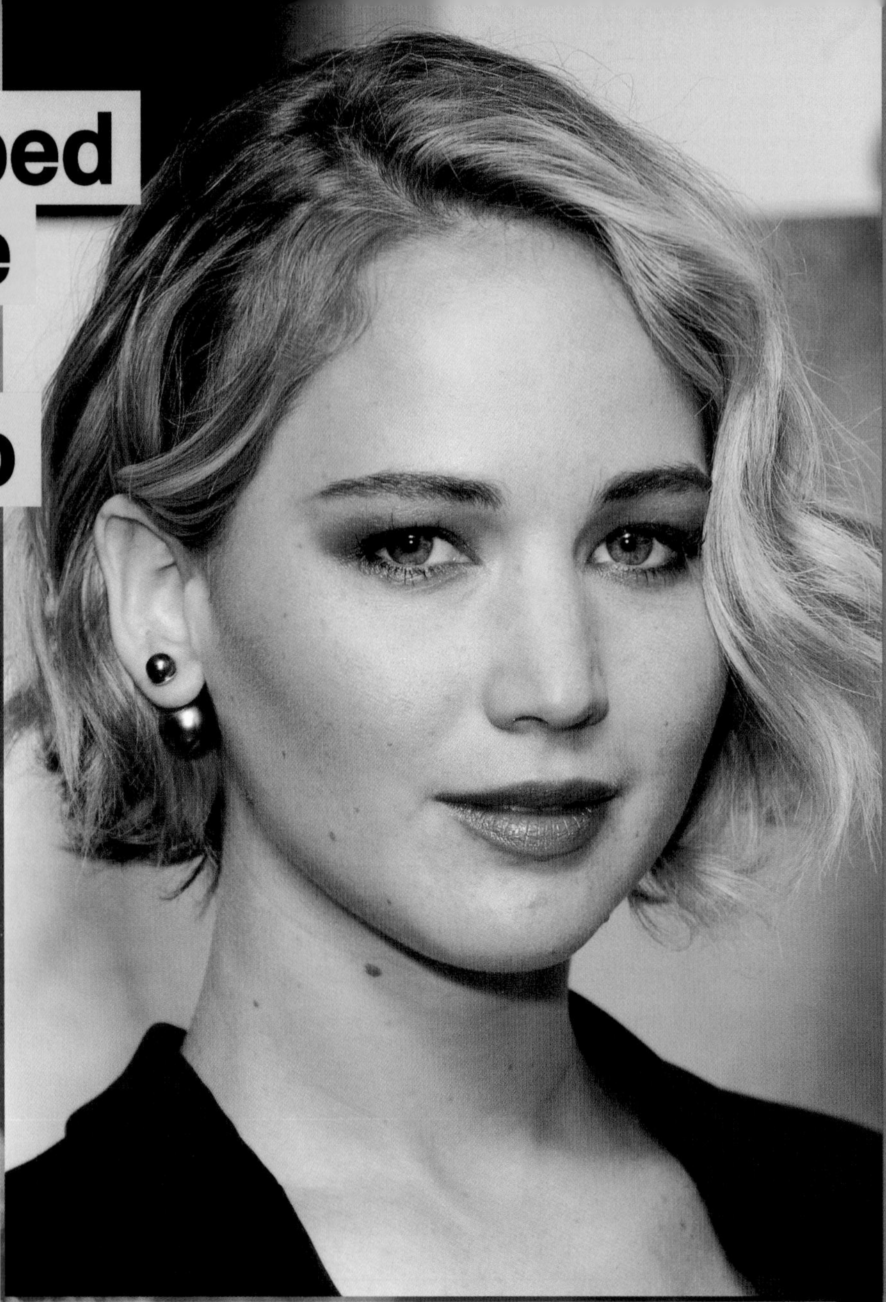

Jennifer Lawrence is probably best known as the revolution-leading heroine Katniss Everdeen from the blockbuster Hunger Games movies. The series cemented Lawrence's standing as a Hollywood leading lady.

Lawrence's big break came when she was cast in the independent film *Winter's Bone*, for which she earned an Oscar nomination. She was only 20 years old. Lawrence went on to play the shape-shifting mutant Mystique in the rebooted *X-Men* films.

In 2013, the star took home the Oscar for Best Actress for her performance in the dramatic comedy *Silver Linings Playbook*. Lawrence, who is known for being a bit of a klutz, tripped on her way to the stage to accept the award. She laughed it off and received a standing ovation.

Because of Lawrence's down-to-earth personality, she's earned the nickname America's Best Friend. Her own friends and cast mates describe her as funny and approachable, and say she has a huge heart. Lawrence's Hunger Games costar Willow Shields told TIME FOR KIDS, "She is so sweet, she's hilarious, she's like a big sister [to me] on set, and I always have a blast filming with her. There's no one else who could play Katniss." ■

Who created Spider-Man and the Hulk?

You might recognize **Stan Lee** because he pops up in almost every Marvel film. If it weren't for Lee, many of the world's most beloved superheroes would not exist today.

The legendary comic titan helped usher Marvel into the silver age of comics. His popular co-creations with artists such as Jack Kirby and Steve Ditko include Spider-Man, the X-Men, the Incredible Hulk, the Fantastic Four, Black Panther (the comic world's first black superhero), Thor, and Iron Man.

Lee joined Timely Comics in 1939 as an office assistant. The company would later become Marvel Comics. In the early 1960s, competitor DC Comics had a hit title: Justice League of America. Marvel wanted to create something that could rival it. That's when Lee and Kirby got the idea for the Fantastic Four. The series, which debuted in November 1961, helped establish Marvel as a comic- book giant.

Even though his characters had amazing powers, Lee was known for giving them a sense of humor and humanity as well. His comics tackled real-world themes, like dealing with the loss of loved ones, prejudice, and war. This would influence other comics for years to come. ■

Who is the acclaimed author of the Harry Potter series?

Harry Potter, the fictional boy wizard, is widely celebrated by fans across the globe—and so is his creator, **J.K. Rowling**. The British author rose to international fame with the release of her magical, best-selling series about Harry Potter and his friends. The seven-book series has been distributed in more than 200 territories, translated into 68 languages, and has sold more than 400 million copies worldwide.

Rowling got the idea for the story on a crowded train traveling from Manchester to London, England, in 1990. As she tells it, "the idea for Harry Potter simply fell into my head." She didn't have a pen to write down her thoughts—and was too shy to ask to borrow one—so she went over the details in her mind. "I simply sat and thought, for four (delayed train) hours, while all the details bubbled up in my brain, and this scrawny, black-haired, bespectacled boy who didn't know he was a wizard became more and more real to me," Rowling later explained on her website. She started writing the first book, *Harry Potter and the Philosopher's Stone*, that same night.

Rowling spent the next five years writing the book and plotting the rest of the series. But getting someone to believe in her work proved difficult. After several rejections from publishers, Bloomsbury Children's Books published *Harry Potter and the Philosopher's Stone* in June 1997. (U.S. audiences know the book as *Harry Potter and the Sorcerer's Stone.*) It was then that Rowling adopted the name J.K. The "J" stands for Joanne, her first name, and the "K" for Kathleen, her grandmother's name. Her publisher thought an obviously female name would not appeal to the book's target audience—young boys.

As it turned out, Rowling's wizarding tales were popular with both boys and girls, and with kids and adults. Each of the eight films that followed, which starred Daniel Radcliffe as Harry Potter, were phenomenal box-office successes. Now there are theme parks, studio tours, and endless amounts of merchandise dedicated to the boy wizard and his wonderful world. ■

You Should Also Know ...

Veronica Roth, author of *Divergent*

• Veronica Roth was only 21 years old when she wrote *Divergent*, the first installment in her young-adult book trilogy. When the book was published, in May 2011, it spent 11 straight weeks on the best-seller list. Readers of all ages adored the book's protagonist, Tris Prior.

Divergent, along with the other two books in the saga, *Insurgent* and *Allegiant*, was a wild success. The trilogy sold 6.7 million copies worldwide in 2013 alone. The series' popularity also led to Hollywood. The *Divergent* movie, starring Shailene Woodley as Tris, hit theaters in March 2014 and made more than $288 million worldwide.

What's the secret to success at such a young age? On her blog, Roth has offered these pieces of advice to aspiring writers: "Learn to love criticism," "Be persistent," and "Be patient."

Who was the top-earning female recording artist of 2014?

People call **Beyoncé Knowles** Queen Bey. The pop/R&B singer is pop-culture royalty. In 2014, Beyoncé ruled the music world as the highest-paid female artist of the year, out-earning runner-up Taylor Swift by $51 million. *Forbes* estimates that Queen Bey earned $115 million between June 2013 and June 2014.

In 2013, the singer spent the year traveling the globe on her massive Mrs. Carter Show World Tour. That December, she also surprised fans by dropping her new, top-secret album online—along with 17 accompanying music videos—without any promotion beforehand. The self-titled fifth solo album shot straight to Number 1, and quickly went platinum. Three months after completing the Mrs. Carter Show tour, Beyoncé embarked on the sold-out On the Run world tour with her husband, rapper Jay Z.

Born September 4, 1981, Beyoncé grew up entertaining crowds in her hometown of Houston, Texas. At age 7, she entered her first talent contest. She blew the competition away, singing John Lennon's "Imagine." A few years later, she joined the group Girls Tyme, which included future Destiny's Child members Kelly Rowland, LeToya Luckett, and LaTavia Roberson.

Beyoncé (left) poses with the members of Destiny's Child.

In 1996, they were signed to Columbia Records, and Destiny's Child was officially born. The group's popularity soared with hit singles, including the Grammy-winning "Say My Name." Luckett and Roberson later left Destiny's Child, and Michelle Williams and Farrah Franklin stepped in.

Beyoncé broke out on her own in 2003. Her first solo effort, *Dangerously in Love*, earned five Grammys in 2004, which tied the record for the most wins ever for a female artist. And they wouldn't be her last. In 2010, Queen Bey set records again when she took home six Grammys, becoming the only female artist to win six trophies in a single show.

Between touring, making new music, and starring in films, the singer also shines in her role as a mom. She and Jay Z welcomed a daughter, Blue Ivy, on January 7, 2012. When Beyoncé accepted the Michael Jackson Video Vanguard Award at the MTV Video Music Awards in 2014, her family was on stage to honor her. "I'm so full," she said. "I have nothing to say, but I'm filled with so much gratitude. I'll just thank God for this moment." ■

● Henson's creations Kermit and Miss Piggy starred in the 1981 film *The Great Muppet Caper*.

Who created the Muppets?

Known for his work on *The Muppet Show* and *Sesame Street*, pioneer puppeteer **Jim Henson** elevated the art of puppetry and created some of pop culture's most famous puppets.

Henson first caught the creative bug while growing up in Mississippi. He was especially close with his maternal grandmother, whose hobbies included painting, quilting, and needlework. She encouraged her grandson's artistic talent.

When Henson was in fifth grade, his family moved to Maryland. In high school, he began performing with his puppets on a local TV program. By his freshman year at the University of Maryland, Henson had his own twice-daily puppet show on local television. The program, *Sam and Friends*, introduced many groundbreaking technical ▶

tricks in puppetry, including angling the TV camera to keep the puppeteer out of the frame instead of having the human hide behind a structure. It also introduced an early version of Henson's best known Muppet, Kermit the Frog, who Henson himself voiced.

Sam and Friends' success led to appearances on national shows, helping Henson's fame grow. In 1966, television producer Joan Ganz Cooney began work on a new educational children's TV program, *Sesame Street*, which premiered in 1969. Cooney asked Henson to create Muppet characters especially for the show. The master puppeteer gave life to Bert and Ernie, Oscar the Grouch, Grover, Cookie Monster, and Big Bird.

But Henson wanted the Muppets to reach a wider audience. In 1975, he partnered with a studio in London, England, to create *The Muppet Show*. The variety show was hosted by Kermit the Frog and featured a new crop of Muppets, including Miss Piggy, Fozzie Bear, Animal, and Gonzo. Celebrity guest stars appeared each week. The show earned three Emmy Awards.

The Muppets also starred in six feature films between 1979 and 1999. (A decade later, the characters would make a triumphant return to the big screen with the release of Disney's *The Muppets,* in 2011, and *Muppets Most Wanted*, in 2014.) From 1984 to 1991, fans also fell in love with the Emmy-winning animated TV spin-off, *Muppet Babies.*

In 1983, Henson introduced the colorful underground creatures of his new TV series *Fraggle Rock*, which aired for five seasons. Henson also directed the fantasy films *The Dark Crystal* and *Labyrinth*. The movies, which combined puppetry with animatronics in a new way, became cult classics.

Henson died unexpectedly on May 16, 1990, following a brief illness. The entire world mourned his loss. His funeral included a moving musical tribute from his Muppets, including a version of Kermit's signature song, "It's Not Easy Being Green," performed by Big Bird. The Jim Henson Company and Jim Henson's Creature Shop carry on his vision and legacy today. ■

Henson gets a hug from his friends, the cast of *Fraggle Rock*.

Who is the Oscar-winning director behind *Jaws, E.T.*, and *Indiana Jones*?

Steven Spielberg is one of the most influential filmmakers of all time. *Jaws*, *E.T. the Extra-Terrestrial*, *Indiana Jones*, and *Jurassic Park* are just a few of the classics he brought to the big screen.

Spielberg's first job in Hollywood was as an intern in the editing department of Universal Studios. He got the internship by sheer luck. While taking a Universal lot tour, he decided to go exploring. Spielberg's excitement about being on a movie set endeared him to the crew. Instead of kicking him out, they let him come back to observe. He returned every day that summer.

In 1969, Spielberg showed Universal executives his short feature *Amblin'*. They were so impressed that they offered him a job as a TV director. Later, his 1975 horror film, *Jaws*, about a giant killer shark, won three Oscars and was nominated for Best Picture.

Spielberg still rules in Hollywood. In 1994, he won his first Oscar for Best Director for the Holocaust drama *Schindler's List*. He later won another Oscar for *Saving Private Ryan*. In 2014, a fifth *Indiana Jones* movie was announced, with Spielberg set to direct. As an executive producer, he's also involved in the *Jurassic World* sequel, a *Gremlins* reboot, and two *Tintin* sequels. At a press conference in 2012, Spielberg was asked if he was thinking of retiring. His answer: "I have no plans to quit." Moviegoers everywhere rejoice. ■

Who began his musical career at age 4 by impersonating Elvis?

Pop superstar **Bruno Mars** was born Peter Hernandez on October 8, 1985, in Honolulu, Hawaii. He was nicknamed Bruno as a baby. When Mars was young, his family would put on shows around town. They sang classic oldies and did celebrity impersonations. At 4 years old, Mars joined the family business as an Elvis Presley impersonator. He later added Michael Jackson to the mix.

After high school, Mars moved to California to try to make it in the music industry. But success didn't come overnight. Frustrated by his stalled career, Mars turned to songwriting.

Producers loved his upbeat melodies and feel-good lyrics. He quickly became one of the industry's top songwriters, which gave him enough influence to break out on his own. His first song as a recording artist was B.O.B's 2010 hit "Nothin' on You." The track soared to Number 1 on the Billboard charts. By 2014, Mars had sold more than 45 million singles worldwide and won two Grammys.

His popularity brought huge ratings for the 2014 Super Bowl halftime show, which Mars headlined. According to Nielsen reports, the show drew in 115.3 million viewers—more than Madonna's 114 million in 2012 and Beyoncé's 110.8 million in 2013.

But the multi-talented singer-songwriter doesn't take success for granted. "It took me a while to finally get it, but when I got it, I think I got it right," Mars told the Hawaiian publication *MidWeek* in 2010. "And I'm very proud of how my songs are representing me as an artist." ■

Who was the man behind Mickey Mouse?

Animator **Walt Disney** launched an entertainment empire in 1928, when he introduced the world to Mickey Mouse.

Disney Brothers Studios was still a small operation in Hollywood when Disney and his animator Ub Iwerks came up with the character. They created Mickey as a replacement for another popular character they had developed, Oswald the Lucky Rabbit. They had lost the rights for the long-eared star, and Disney was forced to come up with something new. Using Oswald as a starting point, he and Iwerks shortened the character's ears, added some padding around his middle, and *voila*—Mortimer the Mouse was born. (His name was changed to Mickey not long after.)

The first two Mickey Mouse cartoons came and went without notice. But *Steamboat Willie*, a short cartoon featuring Mickey as a steamboat captain, debuted with matching music and sound effects—and was a big hit. Soon after, the studio introduced Minnie Mouse, Donald Duck, Goofy, and Pluto.

The studio released its first feature film, *Snow White and the Seven Dwarfs*, in 1937. The

Disney created Mickey Mouse in 1928. The character was originally named Mortimer.

movie won raves from critics and garnered Disney an honorary Oscar. *Pinocchio*, *Dumbo*, and *Bambi* followed. In the 1950s, Disney gave the world *Cinderella*, *Peter Pan*, *Alice in Wonderland*, and *Sleeping Beauty*. One of the final films Disney produced was *Mary Poppins*, which mixed live action with animation.

Disney, who was known for his ambition, dreamed of opening a theme park where families could actually meet characters like Mickey Mouse. In 1955, Disneyland opened its gates in California. (In 1971, five years after Disney's death, Walt Disney World opened in Florida.) Today, the Walt Disney Company continues to cast its magical spell. ■

You Should Also Know ...

Hayao Miyazaki, famed animator

• Hayao Miyazaki, who has been called the Japanese Walt Disney, built his empire on his unique style of animation and storytelling.

These days, computer-generated animation is common. But Miyazaki—co-founder of Tokyo's famous animation company Studio Ghibli—stands by the traditional hand-drawn technique he's used since 1963.

The Japanese filmmaker is best known for such breathtaking animated feature films as *Princess Mononoke*, *My Neighbor Totoro*, and *Howl's Moving Castle*. The films often address serious themes, including the struggle between good and evil, environmentalism, and war. His 2001 film *Spirited Away*, about a girl who stumbles upon the entrance to the spirit world, took home the Oscar for Best Animated Feature. It was the first anime movie to win an Academy Award.

Who was the first woman to run a major television studio?

Actress and comedian **Lucille Ball** started the television company Desilu Productions with her husband, Desi Arnaz, in 1950. The studio produced hit TV shows, including *Star Trek*, *Mission Impossible*, and *The Lucy Show*. When Arnaz resigned as the studio's president in 1962, Ball took the reins, becoming the first woman to run a major studio, and one of the most powerful women in Hollywood.

The redheaded star was a force to be reckoned with. By the time she and Arnaz started Desilu, the actress had starred in several movies and had a role in the popular radio comedy *My Favorite Husband*. Around this time, CBS approached the actress to recreate her part for TV. Ball would only do the show if Arnaz could take part too. When CBS refused, she walked away. Instead, Ball and Arnaz took their show on the road. When CBS saw how successful the act was, they offered the couple a contract. The name of the new sitcom was *I Love Lucy*.

It debuted in 1951. Audiences adored the show, which tackled all kinds of real-life issues in a humorous way. Nicknamed the Queen of Comedy, Ball wasn't afraid to get messy. If it would get laughs, she would gladly stomp around in a tub of grapes or stuff her mouth full of chocolates. But she never saw herself as a funny person. "I'm not funny," she famously explained. "What I am is brave."

Ball won four Emmys for her work, and was also honored with the Emmy's Governors Award. In 1989, she received the Presidential Medal of Freedom. After *I Love Lucy* ended, she continued to lead Desilu and produce other projects. Though she died in 1989 at the age of 77, millions of people still tune in to see her show in reruns. ■

Who rose to fame on the TV show *Victorious*?

Ariana Grande got her first taste of Hollywood fame playing Victoria Justice's friend and classmate on the TV show *Victorious*. Since stepping into the role of bubbly redhead Cat Valentine on the popular Nickelodeon series in 2010—and then again in the 2013 spin-off sitcom *Sam & Cat*—Grande's star has risen.

Grande is more recognized now for her singing. Her big vocals and throwback sound often get compared to Whitney Houston and Mariah Carey. Grande's first studio album, *Yours Truly*, which was released in 2013, shot straight to Number 1 on the Billboard 200. In 2014, her second album, *My Everything*, also debuted at the top of the charts, giving her two Number 1 albums in less than a year. She has taken home multiple awards for her music, including New Artist of the Year at the 2013 American Music Awards and the 2014 Billboard Rising Star award.

Born on June 26, 1993, the Florida native stepped into the spotlight in 2008. Her performance as Charlotte in the Broadway musical *13* earned her a National Youth Theatre Association Award. Not long after, she won the role of Cat Valentine. Grande's rise was fast, but her star likely won't burn out any time soon. ■

Who wrote *The Cat in the Hat?*

The Cat in the Hat—you know enough about that. What about Dr. Seuss, the man behind the magic?

Dr. Seuss was a pen name. The beloved children's book author was born **Theodor Seuss Geisel**, on March 2, 1904, in Springfield, Massachusetts. He began signing his work as Dr. Theophrastus Seuss while working as a magazine cartoonist in 1927. The following year, he shortened it to Dr. Seuss.

After dozens of rejections, Geisel finally published his first children's book, *And to Think That I Saw It on Mulberry Street*, in 1937. But it was his 1957 book, *The Cat in the Hat*—about a stovepipe-hat-wearing, trouble-making cat—that catapulted him to fame. He wrote the bestselling story to engage beginning readers. Its success inspired Geisel to help launch Beginner Books, a division of Random House devoted to helping young kids learn to read.

Geisel went on to write and illustrate many enduring classics, including *How the Grinch Stole Christmas*, *Green Eggs and Ham,* and *The Lorax*. His vibrant illustrations, signature rhymes, and playful stories enchanted kids and their parents. Their powerful lessons about acceptance, open-mindedness, and believing in yourself spoke to people of all ages.

Dr. Seuss died on September 24, 1991. He was 87 years old. Read Across America is held each year to celebrate Geisel's birthday. Students and educators across the nation honor him by reading his books and wearing red-and-white-striped stovepipe hats. The Cat in the Hat, the Grinch, Horton, the Sneetches, the Whos of Whoville, and all of his treasured characters have proven to have lasting appeal. ■

Dr. Seuss shares a smile with models of some of his characters in 1959.

Who is the Hollywood actress known for her humanitarian work?

Angelina Jolie is as well-known for her tireless humanitarian work as she is for being one of Hollywood's most successful leading ladies. In recognition of her years of service, the United Nations appointed Jolie to be a special envoy, or representative, for the organization in 2012. In this role, Jolie travels the world for the U.N. She works on behalf of refugees, or people who have been forced to flee their countries as a result of disaster or war.

Jolie became interested in the issue in 2000, after filming her adventure movie *Lara Croft: Tomb Raider* on location in Cambodia, where more than 13,000 refugees live. With her eyes newly opened to the problem, Jolie became a Goodwill Ambassador for the United Nations High Commissioner for Refugees (UNHCR) in 2001. She has been raising awareness about the crisis ever since. ▶

● Jolie gives education materials to children in Afghanistan in 2011.

● Jolie presents an award at a 2011 United Nations award ceremony.

▶ Jolie has carried out dozens of field missions all over the globe on behalf of the U.N. She has visited refugee camps in Cambodia, Pakistan, Sudan, Haiti, Iraq, and other countries. Jolie's star power has helped draw much-needed attention to the many challenges facing refugees in these often overcrowded camps.

For her commitment, the U.N. Correspondents Association presented Jolie with the Citizen of the World Award in 2003. Two years later, she received the U.N.'s Global Humanitarian Award. And in 2007, the International Rescue Committee honored Jolie with its Freedom Award.

Her activism is as much a part of her identity as her acting. Jolie's parents, Jon Voight and Marcheline Bertrand, were both actors, so it's in her blood. In 2000, Jolie won her first Oscar, for Best Supporting Actress in the drama *Girl, Interrupted*. She quickly became one of Hollywood's most sought-after talents. But beyond her work in the entertainment industry, Jolie's good deeds will leave a mark on the world stage. ■

You Should Also Know . . .

Audrey Hepburn, actress and humanitarian

• Film and fashion icon Audrey Hepburn is revered for her roles in classic films, including *Breakfast at Tiffany's* and *My Fair Lady*. The star also worked on behalf of the United Nations Children's Fund (UNICEF).

After her appointment as a Goodwill Ambassador for UNICEF in 1989, she found her second career as a humanitarian. Hepburn's first mission was to Ethiopia, where a severe shortage of food was causing much suffering. After the trip, she spoke about what she had seen and the importance of UNICEF's work.

Hepburn made many more trips around the globe on behalf of UNICEF. For her work and dedication, she received the Presidential Medal of Freedom in 1992.

Who is the small-town girl who became the queen of pop?

Not many superstars would invite a group of fans to their home for a private listening party for her new album. Or show up at a fan's house unannounced, bearing gifts. But **Taylor Swift** would—and has. These small but meaningful gestures help make the young singer-songwriter beloved by people around the world.

When she was 14, Swift convinced her family to move to Nashville, Tennessee, so that she could take a stab at stardom. It took persistence for her to get her big break. But her self-titled debut album sold more than 2.5 million copies, and soon Swift was a star.

Swift took both the country music world and the pop world by storm with her crossover hits. She's the first female recording artist to have four consecutive albums spend six weeks or more at the top of the charts. She's won countless honors, including American Music Awards, Billboard Awards, Academy of Country Music Awards, and Grammys. In 2010, she became the youngest person to win a Grammy for Album of the Year, for *Fearless*.

Swift's Red Tour made the most money in country-music history, and her album *1989* was the top-selling album of 2014. Yet with all of her success, she still makes every effort to stay true to herself and her fans. ■

Innov

ators

Who cofounded Apple and transformed the digital world?

Apple cofounder and CEO **Steve Jobs** transformed the tech world with his groundbreaking ideas. Under his leadership, the company introduced the Macintosh computer, the iMac, the iPod, the iPhone, the iPad, and more. Each of these revolutionary products reinvented the way people connect with each other and with media.

Jobs and his friend Steve Wozniak cofounded Apple in 1976, when Jobs was just 21. Personal computers were still new when the two Steves came on the scene. Wozniak's original Apple I computer was sold as a kit that users put together themselves. The following year, they created a complete computer, the Apple II, which quickly became a bestseller.

In 1985, Jobs left Apple and went on to start and invest in new companies, including the animation studio Pixar. He returned to Apple in late 1996.

With Jobs back in the driver's seat, Apple once again became an industry

● **Jobs shows off the Apple II computer in 1979.**

pioneer, introducing the iPod in 2001, the iPhone in 2007, and the iPad in 2010. Apple was back on top, thanks to Jobs's vision.

Jobs's creativity and passion for technology began when he was young. He grew up in Mountain View, California. His father, who worked as a machinist, showed him how to take apart and put together electronics.

Jobs died of a rare cancer in 2011. He never stopped innovating, even while ill, and millions of people mourned his death. Jobs left behind endless inspiration for younger generations. In a speech to Stanford University graduates in 2005, he shared this advice: "Don't let the noise of others' opinions drown out your own inner voice. And most important, have the courage to follow your heart and intuition." ■

Who invented Facebook?

Facebook CEO **Mark Zuckerberg** was only 19 years old when he cofounded the popular social networking site. As a sophomore at Harvard University, in 2004, he developed Facebook in his dorm room. Along with three friends—Dustin Moskovitz, Chris Hughes, and Eduardo Saverin— Zuckerberg first launched the site only for Harvard students. Known then as The Facebook, it became an instant hit. They opened it up to other colleges and universities, and before long, anyone with an email address could start an account.

Zuckerberg left Harvard after his sophomore year to focus on growing the company. He moved operations to Palo Alto, California. By the end of 2004, the site had 1 million users. Today, more than 1 billion people worldwide use Facebook to share news and photos, and to stay connected with friends and family.

Zuckerberg always had a knack for computer programming. At around age 12, he built an instant-messaging system for his father's dental office. As a teen, he and a friend created a music-software program called Synapse, which built personalized playlists based on users' listening habits.

Even with Facebook's success, Zuckerberg remains devoted to helping the site evolve and grow. "I'm one of the luckiest people in the world," he wrote in a post in 2014. "I feel a responsibility to all of you to make every day count and help build the best services for you that I can." ■

Who invented the moving assembly line?

Henry Ford cemented his place in history as the founder of the Ford Motor Company and as the visionary behind the Model T. But his legacy goes beyond automobiles. In late 1913, Ford introduced the use of moving assembly lines to build his cars, which transformed manufacturing practices. Ford's method of mass production is still used today.

Ford started the Ford Motor Company in 1903. At the time, automobiles were difficult and expensive to build. The company built only a few cars a day. Ford wanted to make his vehicles more affordable. In 1908, he achieved that goal with the release of the Model T.

The new car was easy to operate and repair, and cheaper than other cars. Sales quickly skyrocketed. To meet the growing demand for the Model T, Ford and his team had to build it more efficiently. He eventually developed the moving assembly line.

With this new method, workers stayed in one place and performed the same task as vehicles passed by on a conveyor belt. This allowed the company to make more cars at a far lower price. Ford also doubled the workers' wages, to $5 a day. With the pay increase, more of his workers could buy the cars they helped make. Over the next two decades, Ford made more than 15 million Model Ts. By 1922, half of the cars in America were Model Ts.

While the company built its last Model T in 1927, it went on to produce many other popular cars, including the Lincoln Continental and the Mustang. Today, the Ford Motor Company is still one of the largest carmakers in the world. ■

intel

Who is the scientist best known for studying black holes?

Stephen Hawking is considered one of the most brilliant minds in science. An internationally renowned astrophysicist, Hawking is famous for his pioneering research on black holes. He is also an expert on Albert Einstein's theory of relativity, which explains the behavior of objects in space and time. Hawking's papers have shed much light on the mysteries of the universe.

Hawking has always been fascinated by the cosmos. Born in Oxford, England, on January 8, 1942, Hawking studied physics at Oxford's University College. He later earned his doctorate in cosmology, or the study of the universe, at the University of Cambridge.

While at Oxford, Hawking began experiencing problems with his health. He sometimes had difficulty speaking, or he would trip or fall for no apparent reason. Shortly after he turned 21, doctors diagnosed him with amyotrophic lateral sclerosis (ALS), a severe brain and spinal illness that is also known as Lou Gehrig's disease.

Hawking's doctors said he likely had only two to three years to live. But he defied those odds and has lived a full life. After his diagnosis, Hawking worked harder than ever to complete his doctorate and finish his research.

In a way, having ALS pushed Hawking to be the scientist he is today. "Before my condition was diagnosed, I had been very bored with life," he wrote in his memoir. "There had not seemed to be anything worth doing."

Hawking made several discoveries that changed the way scientists view the universe. His most celebrated triumph happened in 1974, when he demonstrated that ▶

Hawking, one of the most brilliant minds in science, gives a lecture in 2008.

▶ black holes release radiation. At the time, it was believed that nothing could escape the tremendous gravitational force of a black hole. This breakthrough, called Hawking radiation, made the young scientist a celebrity.

Hawking now uses a wheelchair and speaks with the aid of a computer, but he still travels the world giving lectures. He's also written many books about space, and has co-authored some children's books with his daughter, Lucy. The 2014 Oscar-nominated film *The Theory of Everything*, starring British actor Eddie Redmayne, tells the story of Hawking's life. ■

You Should Also Know ...

Edwin Hubble, galactic explorer

• Edwin Hubble discovered that there are other galaxies in the universe besides our own Milky Way. He's also famous for noting that the universe is constantly expanding. His findings changed the way scientists studied the cosmos.

In honor of Hubble's important contributions to science, NASA named the Hubble Space Telescope after him. The orbiting telescope was launched into space in 1990, 101 years after Hubble's birth. Since then, it has transmitted hundreds of thousands of images of other galaxies to scientists on Earth.

Who was the only woman to win two Nobel Prizes?

In a field dominated by men, **Marie Curie** was one of the most celebrated scientists of her time. Her work in radioactivity made her the first woman to be awarded a Nobel Prize in physics. She shared the award with her husband, Pierre, and physicist Henri Becquerel. She later won a second Nobel Prize for her work in chemistry, becoming the first (and only, to date) woman to win the prize twice.

Together with Pierre, Curie discovered the chemical elements polonium and radium. Her research led to the development of new weapons and medical treatments, including mobile x-ray machines. During World War I, Curie aided the war effort by equipping ambulances with portable x-ray machines. The vehicles were nicknamed Little Curies. The machines let military doctors diagnose injuries near the battlefield, helping thousands of wounded soldiers.

Curie was born Maria Sklodowska on November 7, 1867, in Warsaw, Poland. She was an excellent student. In 1891, she moved to Paris, France, to study physics and mathematics at the prestigious Sorbonne University.

The many years that Curie spent researching radioactive materials greatly affected her health. Curie died on July 4, 1934, of aplastic anemia, a blood disease often caused by exposure to high levels of radiation. The scientific community would not be where it is today had it not been for Curie's dedication to her work. ■

Who pioneered the cubist art movement?

Born in Málaga, Spain, on October 25, 1881, **Pablo Picasso** became one of the most influential artists of the 20th century. While he was known for different painting techniques, he was most famous for creating a movement called cubism, a style of art in which objects and surfaces are represented by simple shapes.

Picasso and French artist Georges Braque wanted to show the same subject from many angles, all at the same time—but on a flat canvas. To do so, they broke the subject down into different geometric shapes, such as circles and squares, and repainted them from different views. Some of Picasso's most famous cubist paintings include *Three Musicians* and *Girl with a Mandolin*.

When Picasso and Braque began experimenting with cubism, in 1907, it was a far departure from the traditional art forms of the day. The inventive style inspired many other innovations in modern art, including the abstract and surrealist art movements.

Picasso's father, Don José Ruiz y Blasco, was a painter and art teacher. Taking after his father, Picasso was a talented artist even as a young boy. Some say his first words were "piz piz"—an attempt at saying *lápiz*, which is Spanish for pencil. As a teen, Picasso attended two prestigious Spanish art schools. But he grew bored with the classical techniques taught in his classes and longed to create something new and different.

In the early 1900s, Picasso moved to France, where he lived for most of his life. He worked with different mediums and artistic styles. In the late 1920s, Picasso experimented with surrealism. This style of art combines random images, like something you would see in a dream. His most renowned piece from this period is *Guernica*, which depicts the tragedies of the Spanish Civil War during the late 1930s.

Picasso died at age 91, in 1973. His masterpieces remain some of the most treasured pieces in the art world. ■

Three Musicians **is one of Picasso's most famous cubist works.**

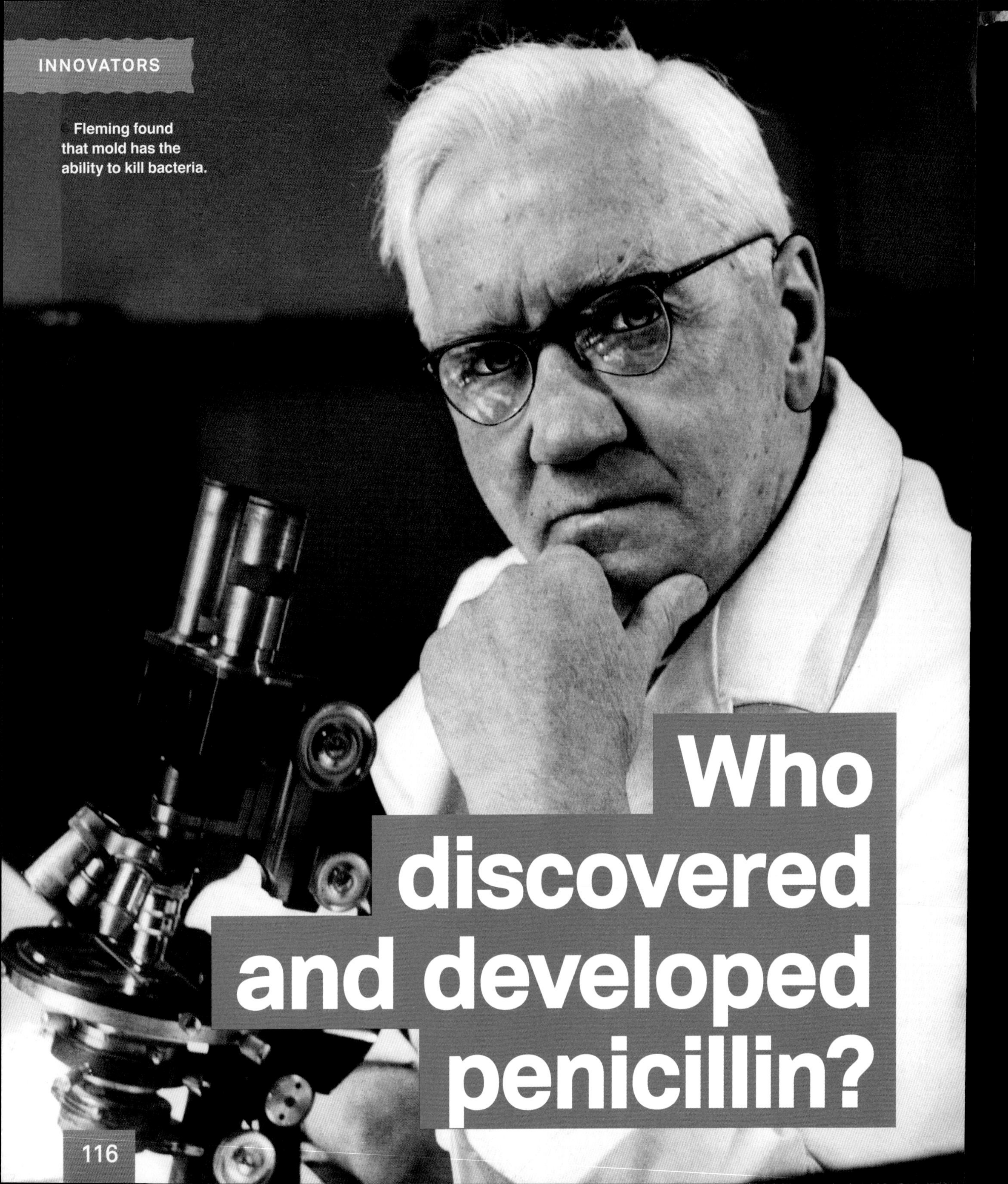

Fleming found that mold has the ability to kill bacteria.

Who discovered and developed penicillin?

Scientists Florey (left), Chain (shown here), and Heatley (not pictured) developed penicillin.

It was an accident! **Sir Alexander Fleming** discovered the antibiotic penicillin by chance, in 1928. The inadvertent discovery changed modern medicine and continues to save countless lives.

Fleming was a young bacteriologist working at St. Mary's Hospital in London, England, when he made the groundbreaking discovery. He had just returned to the lab after a vacation in Scotland. He was examining petri dishes of bacteria samples when he noticed mold on one of his cultures. Looking at the sample under a microscope, Fleming was surprised to see that the mold had killed much of the bacteria. After further tests, he found it had the ability to kill several different strains of harmful bacteria. He had stumbled upon the world's first antibiotic.

The discovery marked a huge turning point in medicine. At the time, there was no drug treatment for deadly bacterial infections. Penicillin had the potential to change that. Unfortunately, Fleming didn't have the resources or the chemistry background to research and develop the drug.

Nearly 10 years later, in 1938, **Dr. Howard Florey** and his colleagues at Oxford University turned the penicillin mold into a lifesaving wonder-drug. Florey had read Fleming's paper on the penicillin mold, and he and his colleagues **Dr. Ernst Chain** and **Dr. Norman Heatley** began growing huge amounts of the mold to conduct experiments. After a few years of research, the medicine was ready to be introduced to the world.

Antibiotics were first used by the military during World War II. The medicine drastically reduced the number of deaths caused by bacterial infections on the battlefield. Florey and Heatley worked with companies in the U.S. to mass-produce the drug.

For their contributions, Fleming, Florey, and Chain were awarded the 1945 Nobel Prize in Physiology or Medicine. For his role, Heatley was honored by Oxford University. Today, penicillin is one of the most widely used antibiotics in the world. ■

Who built the world's first successful airplane?

Wilbur and Orville Wright defied gravity when they built and flew the world's first successful engine-powered airplane. After many years of careful research, planning, and testing, the brothers took their historic flight on December 17, 1903, in Kitty Hawk, North Carolina.

At the time, flying seemed far-fetched. But the Wright brothers were determined to find a way. Wilbur and Orville were fascinated by aeronautics—the science of flight. They realized they needed to build a powered plane that could be controlled. They experimented with different models and observed birds to

try to copy the position of their wings in flight. After each trial, the brothers evaluated the data and made changes based on their findings. Finally, they were ready to test their first flying machine.

The duo chose Kitty Hawk for its strong winds, hills, and sandy dunes. They assembled their plane, the *Flyer I*, on site. It weighed 600 pounds and had a wingspan of 40 feet. On that extraordinary day, the brothers flipped a coin to see who would make history first. Orville won the toss, and climbed into the pilot's seat. Wilbur helped push the plane down a wooden ramp. The plane lifted into the air, staying up for 12 seconds and traveling 120 feet. Success! They flew three more flights that day. During the final flight, Wilbur stayed airborne for 59 seconds and traveled 852 feet.

The brothers did flying demonstrations across the country and in Europe. Wilbur and Orville were constantly trying to improve their design. Over the next two years, they built the *Flyer II* and the *Flyer III*. On October 5, 1905, Wilbur set a record while piloting the *Flyer III*. He flew more than 24 miles in 39 minutes.

The brothers became fascinated with flying when they were young boys after heir father brought home a toy helicopter. But before they began experimenting with airplanes, the brothers owned a print shop and then a bicycle shop. In 1909, they started the Wright Company, which built planes for the U.S. military.

Wilbur contracted typhoid fever and died in 1912. Shortly after, Orville retired from the flying business. Considered the fathers of modern aviation, the Wright brothers never stopped reaching for the sky. ■

Chanel, posing in her apartment in Paris, France, in 1950, started her career selling hats.

Who changed the fashion industry?

Coco Chanel made a bold impression on women's fashion with her simple and practical designs. The French designer created an entirely new look for women in the 1920s and 1930s. Today, Chanel is a premiere luxury brand, proving that her style has stood the test of time.

Gabrielle "Coco" Chanel was born on August 19, 1883, in Saumur, France. After her mother died, Chanel was sent to an orphanage. The nuns there taught her to sew—a skill that helped her become one of the most celebrated fashion icons of all time.

Chanel opened her first shop in Paris, France, in 1913. Two more followed, in Deauville and Biarritz. In the beginning, she sold hats. For extra warmth one chilly day, Chanel fashioned a dress out of jersey material. She received scores of compliments, and people kept asking her where she had gotten it. That's when she realized she could make a business of selling clothes.

Chanel was the first designer to use jersey, a knit fabric suited to the relaxed style of her pieces. Her creations were considered revolutionary at the time. The designs moved sharply away from the confining corsets women had been wearing and allowed for more comfort. Many of her clothes were inspired by menswear, including her signature cardigan jacket. One of her most timeless contributions to fashion was her trademark "little black dress", which she introduced in 1926. Her perfume line, including the bestselling Chanel No. 5, also remains a classic.

When World War II broke out in 1939, Chanel was forced to close her business. She briefly served as a nurse. After many years away from fashion, the legendary designer made a triumphant return to the industry in 1954.

Chanel worked until her death in 1971. Led by designer Karl Lagerfeld since 1983, the brand continues to be at the forefront of women's fashion. And with a legacy that has spanned more than 100 years, fans of the fashion house can always count on one thing: Chanel never goes out of style. ■

Crick (above) and Watson (right) helped the world understand how genes pass between generations.

Who discovered the double-helix structure of DNA?

James Watson and **Francis Crick**, along with Maurice Wilkins, won the Nobel Prize in Physiology or Medicine in 1962 for their discovery of the double-helix structure of DNA. The breakthrough was one of the most significant scientific findings of the 20th century.

DNA stands for deoxyribonucleic acid. It is the chemical that carries the structure for all living things. For example, our DNA determines things like how tall we are and the color of our hair. It's like an instruction manual for our cells. Before the 1950s, scientists had an inkling that a person's DNA was linked to his or her traits. But they didn't know the structure of DNA, so they didn't fully understand how it worked.

Watson and Crick met at Cavendish Laboratory, in Cambridge, England, in 1951. They had both come to the lab to study the structure of DNA. Watson and Crick ▶

● This illustration shows Watson (right) and Crick working on a model of the DNA double helix.

► became fast friends and put their heads together to unravel this mystery. In a different lab, scientists Maurice Wilkins and Rosalind Franklin were working to solve the same puzzle.

At the time, scientists had already learned a lot about genetics, the branch of biology that deals with inherited traits in living organisms. Applying what was already known about DNA, Watson and Crick got to work. They used sticks and balls to make models of what they thought DNA might look like. They also studied x-ray photos of DNA molecules taken by Wilkins and Franklin. The images were crucial to their research.

After two years of testing, Watson and Crick created an accurate model of DNA. The structure was a twisting double helix, or a spiral shaped like a twisted ladder. They wrote about their discovery in the science journal *Nature*. With this crucial piece of the DNA puzzle in place, scientists finally understood how genes are passed from one generation to the next. ■

You Should Also Know ...

Rosalind Franklin, unsung chemist

• James Watson and Francis Crick owed a huge debt of gratitude to chemist Rosalind Franklin. The x-ray photos she took of the DNA molecule, in addition to those taken by her colleague Maurice Wilkins, played an important role in their findings.

But she never knew of her role in this big breakthrough. Wilkins had shown one of her images to Watson and Crick without telling her. They used her photo in their research without her permission. Sadly, she died four years before Watson, Crick, and Wilkins won the Nobel Prize for their discovery.

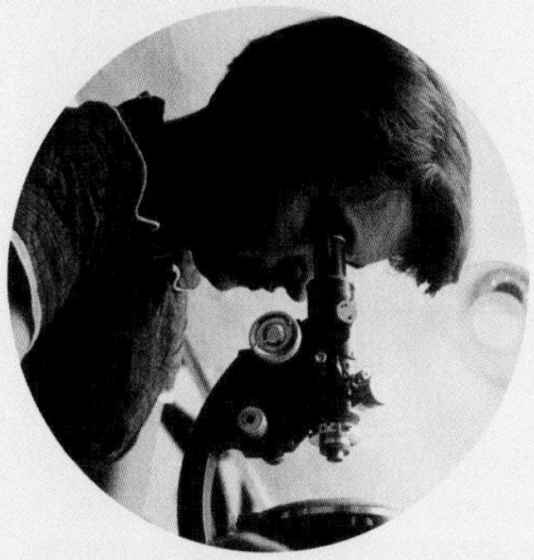

Who founded YouTube?

What do Justin Bieber, the Keyboard Cat, Michelle Phan, and scores of other stars have in common? They all shot to fame because of YouTube. **Steve Chen**, **Chad Hurley**, and **Jawed Karim** founded the video-sharing website in February 2005, in San Bruno, California. It quickly revolutionized the way people view videos and connect on the Internet. YouTube lets anyone with an account easily upload personal videos and share them online. Users post everything from video blogs and funny clips of their cats to tutorials and musical performances on the site. Some people even become famous from it.

YouTube's creators became celebrities, too. The trio had worked together previously at another Internet startup, PayPal. The story of the inspiration behind YouTube changes depending on who you ask. According to Chen and Hurley, the idea was born from their frustration over sending large video files over email. Karim says it sprang from his own frustration over trying to find videos of news events online.

Karim posted the very first video, titled "Me at the zoo," to the site on April 23, 2005. The 18-second clip shows Karim at the San Diego Zoo.

YouTube grew wildly from there. When Google bought the site in 2006, YouTube was attracting more than 700 million views a week. Today, the site boasts more than 1 billion users who upload about 300 hours of video every minute, and watch hundreds of millions of hours of video each day. ■

Who developed the theory of relativity?

Albert Einstein is widely recognized for his genius, and is best known for his theory of relativity. The concept, which he called his masterpiece, changed people's understanding of the universe.

So, what is Einstein's theory of relativity? Put very simply, it explains the behavior of objects in space and time. Einstein came up with the notion in the early 1900s. The papers he wrote describing his theory included new ideas about gravity, energy, time, and light. He also conceived the equation $E = mc^2$. The famous formula suggests that matter can be converted into huge amounts of energy.

Born in Ulm, Germany, on March 14, 1879, Einstein was around 5 years old when his father showed him a compass. He was captivated by the invisible force that caused the needle to move. This curiosity sparked his passion for physics.

Young Einstein questioned everything—even theories that were well established by other scientists (some of which he eventually proved to be incorrect). His papers on relativity made him a celebrity in the academic world, and he traveled the globe giving lectures. In 1921, he won a Nobel Prize in Physics, though it wasn't for his relativity theory.

In December 1932, Einstein took a position at the Institute of Advanced Study, in Princeton, New Jersey. He spent the rest of his life in the U.S. In addition to his devotion to science, Einstein was also a humanitarian. He used his fame to bring attention to human-rights issues around the world. Having experienced discrimination for being Jewish, Einstein became a staunch civil-rights advocate, too. "In the last analysis," he wrote in a letter in 1935, "everyone is a human being." ■

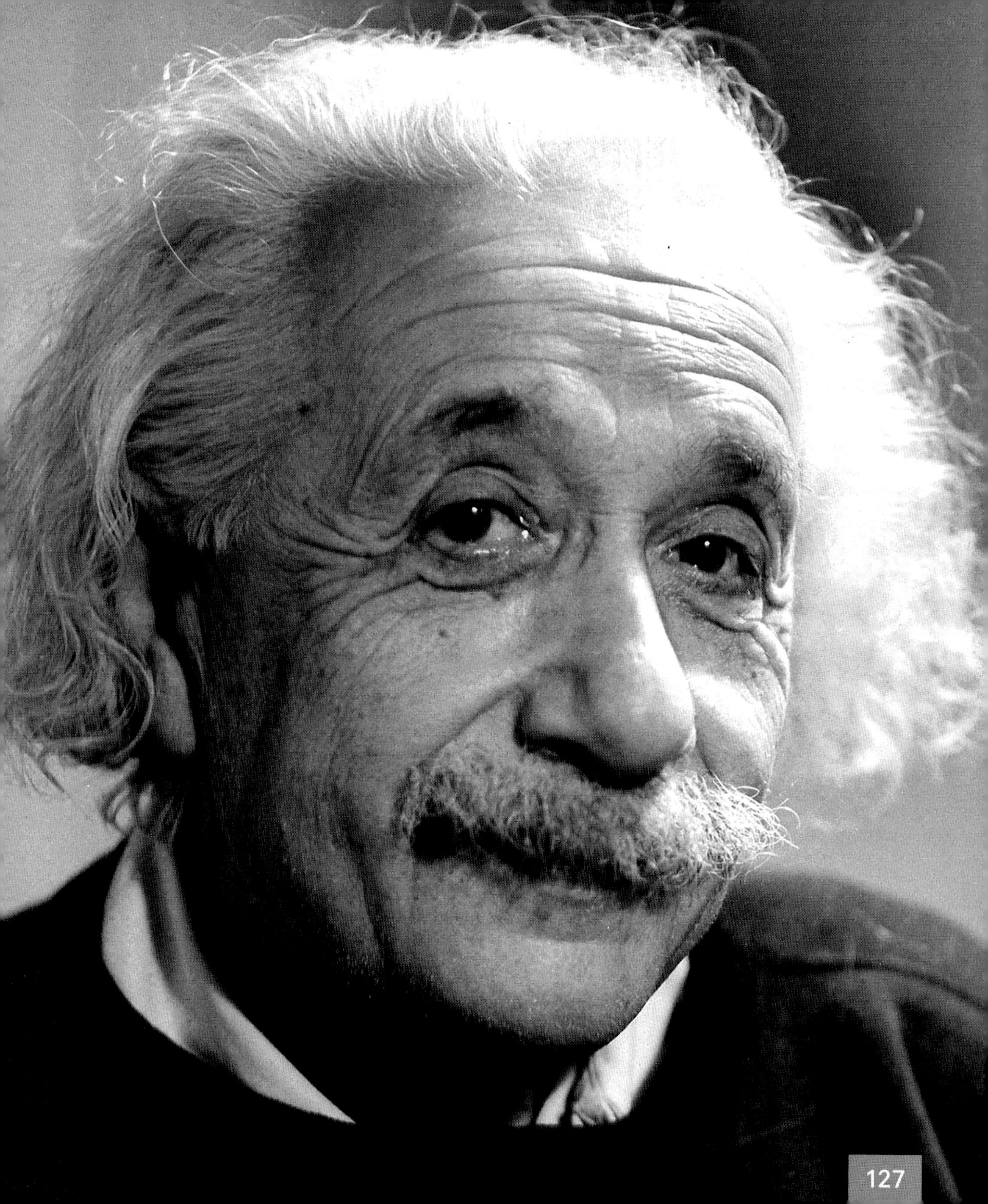

Who was the King of Rock 'n' Roll

The 1950s marked the dawn of rock 'n' roll—and **Elvis Presley** was the King. The handsome singer burst onto the entertainment scene at age 19. His signature performance style, in which he shook his hips, captivated teen audiences. And his sound, a blend of gospel, blues, and country, was unlike anything people had heard before.

Presley was born on January 8, 1935, in Tupelo, Mississippi. He became music royalty, but started from humble beginnings. Presley grew up in a working-class family. For his 11th birthday, his parents bought him a guitar, which he taught himself to play. He enjoyed singing the gospel music he heard in church and listening to country music on the radio. He also loved listening to his neighbors sing the blues.

The Presley family moved to Memphis, Tennessee, in 1948. In Blues City, a young Presley took his budding talent to the next level. In 1954, a year after graduating from high school, he launched his singing career at Memphis's legendary Sun Records label. His debut single was a sped-up cover version of Arthur "Big Boy" Crudup's "That's All Right." The song was an instant hit, and Presley quickly

Presley wows an audience in Miami, Florida, in 1956.

became a household name around the world. Over the next 20 years, he recorded 40 top-10 songs. Eighteen of those singles shot to Number 1 on the charts, including "Heartbreak Hotel," "Love Me Tender," and "Jailhouse Rock." His music earned 14 Grammy Award nominations, including three wins. He also starred in dozens of successful films.

Presley died in 1977, at his Graceland mansion in Memphis. Five years after his death, Graceland opened its doors to the public. More than 600,000 fans flock there each year to pay tribute to the king of rock 'n' roll. ■

Who helped get rid of polio?

Polio is an infectious disease that affects the nervous system. The highly contagious virus can be deadly. As of now, it can't be cured, but it can be prevented, thanks to **Dr. Jonas Salk**.

During the late 1940s and early 1950s, the frequency of polio outbreaks in the United States increased. Salk developed the first safe and effective vaccine for polio in the 1950s. A vaccine is an injection that is given to prevent certain diseases by helping the body build a natural defense.

Salk began researching a polio vaccine at the University of Pittsburgh in 1947. His work caught the attention of what is now the March of Dimes, a foundation created by President Franklin D. Roosevelt to fight the deadly disease. On April 12, 1955, the vaccine was ready.

It significantly decreased the number of new cases of polio. In the few years before Salk's vaccine became widely available, the number of polio cases in the U.S. was an average of more than 45,000. By 1962, the number of cases fell to fewer than 1,000. The U.S. has been polio-free since 1979.

In 1963, Salk opened the Salk Institute for Biological Studies, where he continued to conduct research on many subjects, including multiple sclerosis, cancer, and AIDS. Salk died in 1995, but his spirit of humanity and discovery continue to fuel the institute. ■

Who was the Mexican painter famous for her self-portraits?

Frida Kahlo is one of Mexico's greatest artists, known primarily for her somber self-portraits and the honesty in her work.

Kahlo was born on July 6, 1907, in Coyoacán, Mexico, three years before the start of the Mexican Revolution. She suffered from crippling medical issues her entire life. When she was 6 years old, she contracted polio, which caused her to be bedridden for nine months and which permanently damaged her right leg. When she finally recovered, she walked with a limp.

In 1925, Kahlo severely injured her spine and pelvis in a bus crash. She spent several weeks in the hospital before returning home to heal. During her recovery, she discovered her passion for painting. She finished her first self-portrait the year after her accident. Using the canvas to reflect her pain and despair, she included herself in 55 of her 143 known paintings.

Despite her disability, Kahlo lived life to the fullest. In 1929, she married Mexican painter Diego Rivera, who is known for his large murals. It is said that each artist considered the other to be Mexico's greatest painter. ■

Who created Twitter?

Like many tech companies in Silicon Valley, the story of Twitter's origin is disputed. But everyone agrees it was a group effort. Among the core team that helped create the popular social media platform are **Jack Dorsey** and **Noah Glass**, and Google veterans **Evan Williams** and **Christopher "Biz" Stone**.

At the time, the group was working on a business venture called Odeo, a podcasting startup. Employees were asked to brainstorm new ideas for the company. As some people tell it, that's when Dorsey told Glass his idea to build a system through which people could update others on their status. They worked with another Odeo developer, Florian Weber, to flesh out the idea before presenting it to Williams and Stone. Glass called it Twttr.

The name eventually became Twitter. On March 21, 2006, at 12:50 p.m., Dorsey sent out the first-ever tweet: "Just setting up my twttr," he wrote. Within a year, the social media site had picked up a lot of steam. People were using the platform to tell their followers about what they were doing and to spread news about things

Twitter was started by (from left) Dorsey, Stone, Williams, and Glass (not pictured).

going on around them. For instance, in January 2009, US Airways pilot Chesley "Sully" Sullenberger was forced to make an emergency landing on the Hudson River in New York. Twitter users broke the news first.

In less than 10 years, Twitter has changed the way people communicate and connect. As of March 2015, 288 million monthly active users sent 500 million tweets every day. Everyone from President Barack Obama to Taylor Swift to everyday folks use Twitter to connect with others all over the world. As it turns out, you can say a lot using just 140 characters. ■

Who was one of the most influential architects of the 20th century?

American architect **Frank Lloyd Wright** created some of the most iconic buildings in the world. His simple work, which was influenced by nature, was distinctly American. Wright's idea of beauty was very different from Europe's ornate style of architecture. Because of his innovative designs, Wright is regarded as one of the greatest architects in modern history.

Wright was born in Richland Center, Wisconsin, on June 8, 1867. His family moved around a lot. They finally settled in Madison, Wisconsin, in 1878. Growing up, Wright loved exploring the natural world, which inspired his revolutionary, organic style.

Wright discovered his passion for architecture while in college at the University of Wisconsin. To help support his family, Wright worked in the university's department of engineering, assisting architect Joseph Silsbee on a project. Wright knew then that he had found his life's calling.

In 1887, he left school and headed to Chicago, Illinois, ►

Wright and his team work with a model of the Guggenheim Museum.

where he worked for Silsbee, and later, acclaimed architect Louis Sullivan. Wright married Catherine Tobin in 1889. They had six children together. The home he built for his family became his studio when he started his own firm in 1893. Wright's houses were often inspired by the American prairie. The popular style featured a long, horizontal design and a simple elegance.

Some of Wright's most celebrated works include the

earthquake-proof Imperial Hotel, in Tokyo, Japan; the Fallingwater residence, built on top of a waterfall in rural Pennsylvania; and the Taliesin, his home in Spring Green, Wisconsin, which he rebuilt twice following two devastating fires. Wright later turned the Taliesin into an architecture school.

One of his final projects was designing the Guggenheim Museum for contemporary art, in New York City. He began the project in 1943, and worked on it for 16 years. With its spiraling ramp and clear dome, the enormous circular building drew criticism at first. But today, it's considered to be one of the 20th century's most important architectural landmarks.

Wright died on April 9, 1959, six months before the Guggenheim's completion. He was 91 years old. ■

You Should Also Know ...

I.M. Pei, master of modern architecture

• Frank Lloyd Wright's work inspired many architects, including celebrated Chinese-American architect I.M. Pei.

Today, Pei is often called the master of modern architecture. Known for his innovative designs, Pei is the brilliant mind behind famous structures including the John F. Kennedy Library, in Boston, Massachusetts; the East Building of the National Gallery of Art, in Washington, D.C.; the Rock and Roll Hall of Fame, in Cleveland, Ohio; and the glass pyramids of the Louvre museum, in Paris, France.

In 1983, Pei was awarded the prestigious Pritzker Architecture Prize. He used the $100,000 prize to start a scholarship fund for Chinese students studying architecture in the U.S.

Sports

Stars

Who is the basketball phenom known as King James?

NBA superstar **LeBron James** has certainly lived up to his high school nickname of King James. The All-Star forward has ruled the basketball court since he was a teenager.

After winning two NBA championships with the Miami Heat, James returned to his hometown team, the Cleveland Cavaliers, in 2014. It was in Cleveland that he started his NBA career in 2003. At age 18, he was the youngest player ever to be the top draft pick. He made an immediate impact in his first year, averaging 20.9 points per game and winning the Rookie of the Year award. By age 28, he had scored 20,000 career points. He was

James, who returned to the Cleveland Cavaliers in 2014, makes a thrilling dunk against the Boston Celtics.

the youngest player ever to reach that milestone.

James had to overcome much adversity growing up in Akron, Ohio. As a boy, he and his mother, Gloria, moved every few months. They stayed on the couches of friends and family as Gloria looked for work. In the summer of 1993, an 8-year-old James was invited to play in a youth football league. James had never played the sport before, but he turned out to be a talented athlete and the team's best player. That fall, one of his coaches offered to let James stay with him and his family. Gloria wanted her son to have stability, so she agreed. Their luck was finally changing.

During the football off-season, James started playing basketball. He excelled in that sport, too. By high school, the hoops phenom was receiving national attention. Thousands came out to watch the prep star play, his games were televised, and he landed on national magazine covers.

Today, James remains one of the biggest stars in the NBA. As of 2014, he had won four NBA Most Valuable Player awards. James does it all: he's a big-time scorer, an incredible playmaker, and a tough defender.

Despite his massive success, James has never forgotten his roots. He regularly gives back to his community, supporting organizations including the Boys & Girls Club of America and the Children's Defense Fund. James and Gloria also established the LeBron James Family Foundation, an organization that helps provide educational and enrichment opportunities to young people. Even though his career is far from over, James has already established himself as an all-time great. ■

Who said he could "float like a butterfly, sting like a bee"?

These famous words became the catchphrase of American boxing icon **Muhammad Ali**. His extraordinary speed and graceful footwork made him one of the greatest competitors ever to set foot in the boxing ring. Light on his feet, Ali would float around, evading his opponents. Yet he packed a powerful, stinging punch.

Born Cassius Marcellus Clay Jr. in Louisville, Kentucky, on January 17, 1942, he changed his name to Muhammad Ali in 1964 after becoming a member of the Nation of Islam.

Ali discovered boxing by chance. When he was 12 years old, someone stole his bicycle. He found a police officer named Joe Martin and told him he wanted to fight the thief. As fate would have it, Martin trained young boxers at a local gym. "Well, you'd better learn how to fight before you start challenging

people," he told Ali.

Ali dedicated himself to training with Martin, and was soon competing for amateur titles. He won several matches and secured a spot on the 1960 U.S. Olympic team. On September 5, 1960—only six years after his bike was stolen—he won the light-heavyweight gold medal.

After the Olympics, Ali began his professional career. He fought many legendary matches over the years. In 1964, he took on heavyweight champion Sonny Liston. In an upset, Ali overpowered Liston to win the world heavyweight championship at age 22.

Ali fought his nemesis, Joe Frazier, in three famous bouts, including one known as the Fight of the Century. That 15-round match resulted in Ali's first professional loss. He beat Frazier in the next two matchups. Ali later retained heavyweight titles when he defeated George Foreman in the Rumble in the Jungle in 1974 and Leon Spinks in 1978, becoming the first three-time heavyweight champion. Ali entered the ring for the last time in 1981, at age 39. He will forever be known as the greatest of all time. ■

Ali, a three-time world heavyweight champion, poses in a bank vault in 1963.

Who became an international hero at the 1936 Berlin Games?

During the 1936 Summer Games, **Jesse Owens** became the first track-and-field athlete to win four gold medals in a single Olympics. While it was a remarkable athletic feat, Owens's accomplishments at the Olympic Games went beyond the world of sports.

The 1936 Olympics were held in Berlin, Germany. Nazi dictator Adolf Hitler believed the Olympics would show that the Aryan (or white) race was superior. He criticized the United States for allowing black athletes to compete. Owens set out to prove Hitler wrong, and did so in spectacular fashion.

Owens took home gold medals in all four of his events: the 100 meters, 200 meters, 4x100-meter team relay, and the long jump. He set three Olympic records, one world record, and tied another world record. But more significantly, Owens showed that people should be judged based on their merits rather than the color of their skin. He became an international hero, remembered for his courage as much as for his athletic ability. ■

You Should Also Know...

Usain Bolt, fastest man alive

• Jamaican sprinter Usain Bolt is known as Lightning Bolt for a good reason. He's fast—really fast. Bolt earned the title of the fastest man alive at age 21, when he took home three gold medals and shattered three world records at the 2008 Beijing Olympic Games. He was the first man in Olympic history to win both the 100-meter and 200-meter races in world-record times.

The next year, Bolt sped to glory at the World Championships in Berlin. There, he cut his 100-meter time to an incredible 9.58 seconds, beating his previous record of 9.69 seconds. At the 2012 London Games, he defended all three Olympic gold medals.

Who put U.S. women's soccer on the map?

● Hamm celebrates after making her penalty kick against China in the 1999 FIFA Women's World Cup final.

Mia Hamm is regarded as one of the best female soccer players in the history of the sport. The legendary athlete spent 17 years playing with the U.S. women's national soccer team, leading it to two FIFA Women's World Cup victories. Her unmatched talent on the field made her extremely popular with soccer fans worldwide. As her international fan base grew, the attention given to women's soccer did, too.

The soccer phenom was born on March 17, 1972, in Selma, Alabama. At 15 years old, Hamm was the youngest woman to play for the U.S. senior squad in 1987. She went on to compete in college for the University of North Carolina, where she helped the Tar Heels win four consecutive NCAA championships.

Hamm led the U.S. team to FIFA Women's World Cup titles in 1991 and 1999, and Olympic gold medals in 1996 and 2004. Over the course of her distinguished career, she smashed many records, the most notable being most international goals scored. Her record of 158 goals stood until U.S. soccer player Abby Wambach broke it in June 2013. In 2001 and 2002, FIFA named Hamm World Player of the Year. She was inducted into the National Soccer Hall of Fame in 2007.

Hamm retired from soccer in 2004, but her legacy continues to inspire new generations of female athletes. ■

Who has won the most NFL MVP awards?

Not only does quarterback **Peyton Manning** hold a record five NFL MVP awards, he is also the league's touchdown king. In October 2014, the Denver Broncos QB broke the NFL all-time touchdown record with his 509th TD pass—besting the career record previously set by Brett Favre.

"I'm very humbled and very honored," Manning told reporters of the achievement. "I've always been a big fan of quarterbacks, whether it's Brett Favre or Dan Marino or John Elway. I'm very honored and humbled to join a pretty unique club."

Without a doubt, Manning's name belongs on that list of all-time great quarterbacks. As the son of former NFL quarterback Archie Manning, Peyton seemed destined to follow in his father's footsteps. Manning was born on March 24, 1976, in New Orleans, Louisiana. Thanks to his father, he grew ▶

▶ up around the game. It didn't take long for the Mannings to become known as the First Family of football. (Peyton's younger brother, Eli, is the quarterback for the New York Giants and has won two Super Bowls to date.)

After setting numerous school records and being named an All-American as a senior at the University of Tennessee, Manning was taken by the Indianapolis Colts with the first overall pick of the 1998 NFL draft. From 1998 through 2010, he led the Colts to eight division championships, two American Football Conference championships, and one Super Bowl victory.

A damaged nerve in his neck sidelined Manning in 2011. Eventually the Colts released their longtime QB. Manning bounced back, however, signing a five-year contract with the Denver Broncos in March 2012. The veteran did not slow down. In 2013, he broke the single-season passing-yards record with 5,477 yards.

"It's amazing what he's done—but then again, it's not," Favre told the Associated Press. "I mean that with all due respect, because of his vigilance and determination. He just has the drive to excellence that has made him special." ■

You Should Also Know . . .

Joe Montana, clutch quarterback

• Football Hall of Fame quarterback Joe Montana was a master of comebacks. In fact, his late-game heroics happened so often that people coined the term Montana Magic.

Montana was taken by the San Francisco 49ers in the third round of the 1979 NFL draft. Just two seasons later, he won the first of his three Super Bowl MVP awards.

Montana was famous for keeping calm under pressure, earning him the nickname Joe Cool—and helping him lead the 49ers to four Super Bowl victories. Perhaps his most famous play was in Super Bowl XXIII, after the 1988 season. He led his team on a late 92-yard drive that resulted in a game-winning touchdown with 34 seconds left on the clock.

Serena (left) and Venus Williams hold up their trophies after winning the doubles final at Wimbledon in 2012.

Who are the tennis-star sisters who have won more than 25 Grand Slam titles?

When tennis stars **Venus and Serena Williams** were growing up in Compton, California, their father, Richard, dreamed that his daughters would become the top tennis players in the world. Richard Williams got more than he had hoped for. Not only have the Williams sisters won more than 25 Grand Slam titles between them, they are credited with forever changing women's tennis.

Venus and her younger sister Serena arrived on the scene as teenagers in the late 1990s. The Williams sisters brought a powerful game that the sport had never seen before. With their sheer strength and athleticism, they dominated the women's tour for decades.

In February 2002, Venus became the first African-American woman in the Open Era (which began in 1968) to achieve a Number 1 ranking. She has won five Wimbledon singles titles and two U.S. Opens.

Serena is regarded as one

of the greatest female tennis players of all time. She finished 2014 at the top of the world rankings—the fourth time she has ended the year at Number 1. With a whopping 19 Grand Slam titles, she was four away from the most in the Open Era, as of January 2015.

As doubles partners, the sisters make a mighty pair. They have won 13 Grand Slam doubles titles and three Olympic gold medals. Venus and Serena have also each won an Olympic gold medal in the women's singles tournament. That gives them a record four gold medals apiece.

Between 1994 and 2014, the sisters faced off 25 times in various tournaments, including eight Grand Slam finals. Serena has an edge over her big sister, winning 14 of the matchups. But while they are fierce competitors, they remain supportive of each other. When one sister is competing, the other can usually be seen watching from the stands. After all, for the Williams sisters, tennis is a family affair. ■

Who led the Chicago Bulls to six NBA championships?

Ask a basketball fan to name the greatest player ever and most will answer—without hesitation— **Michael Jordan** . His Airness was a high-flying superstar who dunked with ease, evaded even the toughest defenders, and always came through in the clutch. During his impressive career, Jordan led the Chicago Bulls to six NBA titles (three-peating twice, from 1990–91 to 1992–93 and 1995–96 to 1997–98). He was named the NBA's Most Valuable Player five times. A 14-time All-Star, he also won the All-Star Game MVP award three times. Jordan's career average of 30.1 points per game is the best of all time.

Born February 17, 1963, Jordan famously didn't make his high school varsity basketball team when he was a sophomore. But he soon developed into a star, playing in college at the University of North Carolina. During the 1982 NCAA tournament, he sunk the game-winning basket to lead the Tar Heels to the championship. In 1984, he was drafted third overall by the Chicago Bulls and went on to win Rookie of the Year.

Jordan made a name for himself off the court, too. In 1996, he starred in the blockbuster film *Space Jam*. He also earned many endorsement deals. Nike's Air Jordan sneakers first hit shelves in 1984 and remain popular today.

Accolades aside, the mighty Jordan is best remembered for his unmatched power, speed, and flair on the court, hitting shot after shot with his tongue wagging. "There's Michael Jordan and then there is the rest of us," NBA great Magic Johnson once said. ■

Who is the most decorated Olympian?

Given his comfort in the water, **Michael Phelps** might as well be a fish. On July 31, 2012, the U.S. swimmer made history when he won his record 19th Olympic medal, as part of the winning 4 x 200-meter freestyle relay team at the London Games. He knew he had set a new record even before he finished his final lap. "I started smiling," Phelps said after the event. "I don't think I've ever done that in a race before."

Phelps went on to medal three more times in those Olympics, bringing his grand total to 22 medals—18 gold, two silver, and two bronze.

Phelps started taking swimming lessons at age 7. He was scared to put his head in the water at first, but soon felt right at home. After watching the U.S. swimming team compete in the 1996 Olympic Games, Phelps made it his mission to be a master of the pool.

Just four years later, at the 2000 Olympics, 15-year-old Phelps became the youngest U.S. male swimmer to compete in the Olympics in 68 years. It was the start of a career that saw the athlete consistently break his own records and return to the top of the winner's podium—including a record eight gold medals in a single Games at the 2008 Beijing Olympics.

Phelps owes his success in part to his unique physique. He is 6'4" tall but has an arm span of 6'7". Phelps also wears size 14 shoes, making his feet almost like flippers.

Phelps announced his retirement in 2012, but came back to compete two years later. Whether he wins more Olympic medals or not, he's already established himself as the best swimmer the sport has ever seen. ■

Who was the first African-American gymnast to win the Olympic individual all-around event?

Douglas's gravity-defying moves on the uneven bars inspired her nickname, the Flying Squirrel, before the 2012 Olympics.

While many U.S. athletes shined at the 2012 Olympic Games, perhaps the biggest star to emerge was **Gabrielle Douglas**. The 16-year-old made headlines when she became the first African-American gymnast to take Olympic gold in the individual all-around event. As part of the Fierce Five, Douglas also won a team gold medal with her teammates Aly Raisman, Kyla Ross, McKayla Maroney, and Jordyn Wieber—the first team gold for the U.S. since 1996. The wins made Douglas the first U.S. gymnast to grab gold in both the individual all-around and team competitions in a single Olympics.

Nicknamed the Flying Squirrel for her gravity-defying moves, Douglas first discovered her talent for performing flips as a toddler. Her older sister, Arielle, was a former gymnast and competitive cheerleader. When Douglas was 3, Arielle taught her how to do a cartwheel. That lesson changed her life forever.

Douglas began her formal training at age 6 at a local gym in her hometown of Virginia Beach, Virginia. She proved to be a natural. Just two years later, she was crowned the 2004 state champion. Douglas was determined to reach even higher—she wanted to be a world champion. At age 14, she convinced her family to let her move to Iowa to train with ►

renowned coach Liang Chow, who coached Olympic gold medalist Shawn Johnson.

Under his guidance, Douglas grew into a powerful competitor. In 2011, she earned a team gold at the World Championships. The next year, she placed first at the U.S. Olympic trials, securing a spot on the 2012 U.S. Olympic team. She bested teammate and then-world champion Wieber by one-tenth of a point to guarantee her place.

Douglas became the second black gymnast to be a member of the U.S. Olympic team, after Dominique Dawes's Olympics debut in 1992. Later that year, Douglas proved herself again, this time on the world stage in London, England.

"It felt so amazing," she told TIME FOR KIDS about winning the all-around. "I didn't really think about winning. I just thought about being the best I could be on that day and showing everyone what I was capable of doing. Win or lose, I could still go home, no regrets, and say I gave it my all, 100%, and that I am an Olympian."

As for going after your

dreams, she advises, "If you have the heart, the passion, the drive, the love for it… don't let anyone stop you. Keep fighting and always have fun—that's always important." ■

You Should Also Know …

Mary Lou Retton, America's darling

• The first American to take home gold in the women's gymnastics individual all-around was Mary Lou Retton.

Standing only 4'9", Retton was nonetheless a titan at the 1984 Summer Games. She claimed five medals in those Olympics—the most of any athlete that year. The Virginia native won the all-around competition by a mere 0.05 of a point, thanks to her perfect 10 in her final event, the vault. Retton's masterful performance at the Olympics, not to mention her sparkling personality, catapulted her to stardom. She was featured prominently on a Wheaties cereal box after the 1984 Olympics. Retton was the first woman whose face was put on the front of a Wheaties box. She later became a spokesperson for the brand.

Who was known as the Sultan of Swat?

Babe Ruth had many nicknames during his legendary baseball career. Even Babe was a nickname. He was born George Herman Ruth Jr. on February 6, 1895. People also called him the Sultan of Swat and the Great Bambino. Why? When the super slugger was at bat, chances were good he was going to knock it out of the ballpark.

Ruth ruled major-league baseball from the moment he stepped onto the diamond at age 19. He played his first game, with the Boston Red Sox, on July 11, 1914. He's best remembered as a slug-

ger, but he started his career as an imposing pitcher. In 1916, he led the league with a 1.75 ERA and ranked third with 170 strikeouts. The following season, he led the league with an astounding 35 complete games.

When he got a chance at the plate, he didn't waste it. Recognizing Ruth's hitting talent, the Red Sox decided that Ruth was more valuable as an everyday player. He didn't disappoint. In 1918, he led the league with 11 home runs and led the Red Sox to a World Series win. Then in 1919, he set a major-league record with 29 home runs.

So it came as quite a surprise when Boston sold its best player to the New York Yankees in 1920. The move would haunt the Red Sox for the next 85 years. After Ruth left Boston, the Red Sox didn't win another World Series until 2004. This decades-long drought was known as ▶

► the Curse of the Bambino.

The Yankees, on the other hand, became baseball's best team—and Ruth continued to rewrite the record books. By then, Ruth had made the switch to full-time outfielder. During his first year in New York, he hit 54 home runs, shattering his own record. The following year, he topped it again with 59 home runs. In 1927, he swatted a monster 60 homers, a record that stood until 1961.

During his 15 seasons as a Yankee, the slugger helped his team win four World Series titles and seven American League pennants. He was such a huge part of the team's success that when the Yankees moved to their new stadium in 1923, they called it the house that Ruth built.

Ruth retired from baseball in 1935 with 714 homers, a record not broken until 1974.

Ruth was one of the first

five players inducted into the Baseball Hall of Fame, in 1936. He once said, "Baseball was, is, and always will be to me the best game in the world." For generations of baseball fans, Babe Ruth was, is, and always will be the best ballplayer in the world. ■

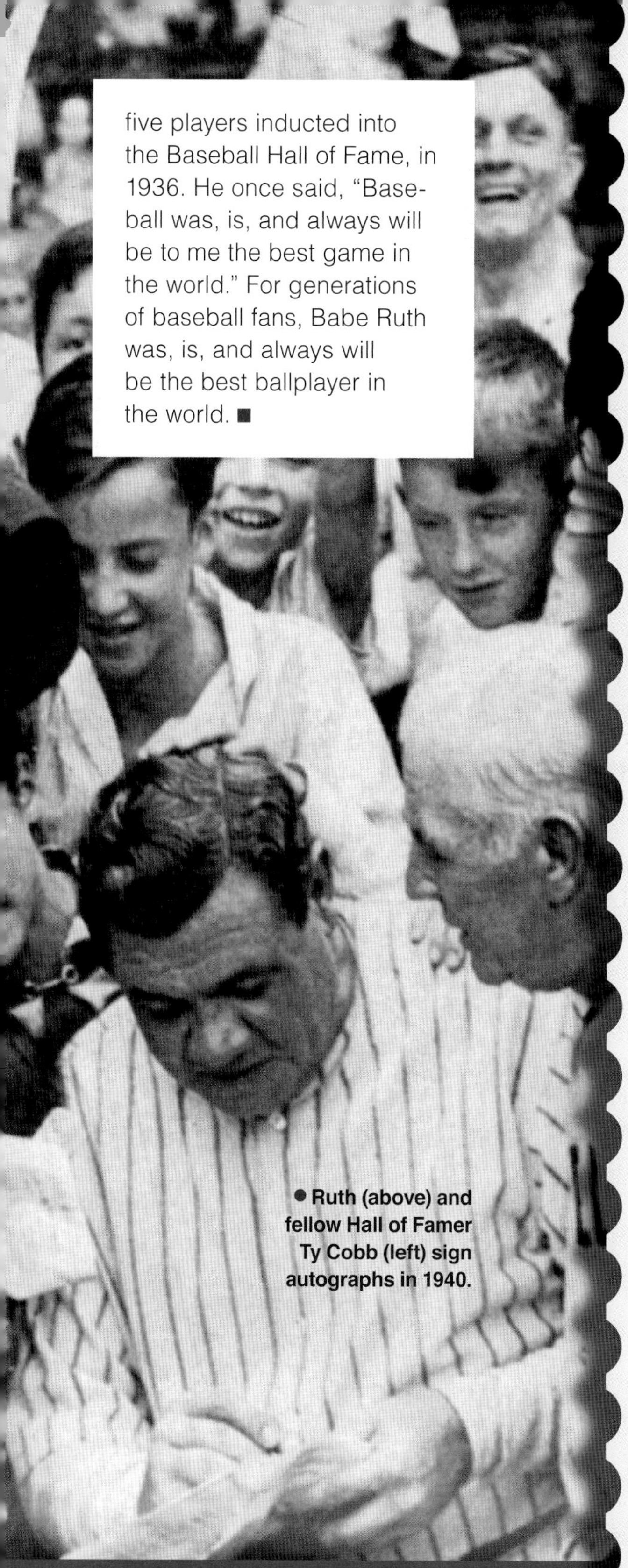

• Ruth (above) and fellow Hall of Famer Ty Cobb (left) sign autographs in 1940.

You Should Also Know . . .

Lou Gehrig, the Iron Horse

• One of Babe Ruth's legendary teammates was first baseman Lou Gehrig. From June 1, 1925, to April 30, 1939, Gehrig never missed a game. He played in a remarkable 2,130 consecutive games, a record that stood until 1995. His endurance and power at the plate led to his nickname, the Iron Horse.

In 1934, Gehrig won baseball's Triple Crown. He led the league with 49 homers, a .363 batting average, and 165 runs batted in. Gehrig won six World Series titles.

But his legacy was cut short when he was diagnosed with ALS, a rare disorder that later became known as Lou Gehrig's disease. In his famous retirement speech, he said, "I consider myself the luckiest man on the face of this Earth."

Who was the youngest NHL captain to win a Stanley Cup?

When hockey great Wayne Gretzky was asked in 2002 which player could challenge his records, his answer was **Sidney Crosby**, a teen-ager who was then dominating the Quebec Major Junior Hockey League. Crosby has lived up to the hype. After being drafted first overall by the Pittsburgh Penguins in 2005, the then-19-year-old became the youngest NHL scoring champion when he finished 2006–07 with 120 points. Crosby was named team captain in 2007–08 and in 2009 led Pittsburgh to the Stanley Cup. At age 21, he became the youngest captain to hoist the Cup. Though Crosby has battled injuries, he was in top form in 2013–14, taking home his second Hart Trophy as league MVP.

Crosby is also an Olympic hero for Canada. During the 2010 Olympic Games in Vancouver, Canada, Crosby scored the gold medal–winning overtime goal against the U.S. He helped his home country defend the gold at the 2014 Sochi Olympics. ■

You Should Also Know . . .

Wayne Gretzky, the Great One

• Wayne Gretzky is widely regarded as the best hockey player in history. And he has the records to prove it. Known as the Great One, he ruled the ice during his 20 years in the NHL. He holds more than 60 league records, including career goals (894), assists (1,963), and points (2,857). Gretzky is also the only NHL player to finish with more than 200 points in a season, a feat he achieved four times. He won four Stanley Cups with the Edmonton Oilers and was named league MVP nine times. After his retirement in 1999, Gretzky was immediately inducted into the Hockey Hall of Fame.

Who was considered the greatest female athlete of the 20th century?

Not many people know about **Babe Didrikson Zaharias** these days. But they should! Named the top woman athlete of the century by the Associated Press in 1999, Didrikson Zaharias excelled in every sport she played—baseball, basketball, swimming, and volleyball, to name a few. One of her greatest achievements came at the 1932 Olympics, where she won two gold medals and one silver competing in track and field. She is most famous, however, for her impact on women's golf.

The outgoing athlete did more than any other player of her era to popularize the sport. She picked up golf in the early 1930s, and as with every other arena, she made it her mission to be the best. Didrikson Zaharias trained for hours every day. She practiced even when her hands became sore and blistered. She quickly mastered the game.

As an amateur golfer in 1946, Didrikson Zaharias won 13 straight tournaments. She followed this impressive streak with another historic feat—becoming the first American to win the British Ladies' Amateur in Scotland, in 1947.

In 1950, Didrikson Zaharias was among the 13 female golfers who helped found the Ladies Professional Golf Association (LPGA). She won 31 events as a pro golfer, including three U.S. Opens. As of March 2015, she still holds the LPGA record for being the fastest player to reach 10, 20, and 30 career wins. ■

Everyday

Heroes

Who became a voice for Holocaust victims when her diary was published?

In her now-famous diary, **Anne Frank** showcased her bravery in the face of horror. The journal of this young Jewish girl, who died during World War II, remains one of the most important and powerful memoirs in history.

In the diary, Anne describes her family's experience hiding from the Nazis, the German political party that tried to wipe out Jewish people. The war lasted from 1939 to 1945, but Nazi discrimination against Jews started years earlier. In what became known as the Holocaust, the Nazis persecuted and killed nearly 6 million Jews, including 1 million children. Anne Frank was one of them.

The Franks were living in Amsterdam, the Netherlands, when German troops invaded in May 1940. Within a few months, the Nazis began enforcing anti-Jewish measures. Jews had to attend separate schools. They weren't allowed to go to the movies. They were banned from owning businesses. And they had to wear yellow stars on their clothes to identify themselves as Jewish.

When Anne's older sister, Margot, received a call to report to a German work camp in July 1942, the Franks knew they had to hide. Anne's father, Otto, had been planning for it. He had already prepared a secret apartment behind his office. The family lived there in secret for more than two years. Otto's business partner, Hermann van Pels, along with his wife, Auguste, and son, Peter, and a dentist named Fritz Pfeffer also joined the Franks in hiding. Meanwhile, at great risk to themselves, Otto's friends and office workers smuggled in food, clothing, and books for the families.

While hiding in the secret annex for 25 months, Anne used her diary, a gift from her ▶

Anne, at age 11, writes in a journal at school in the Netherlands.

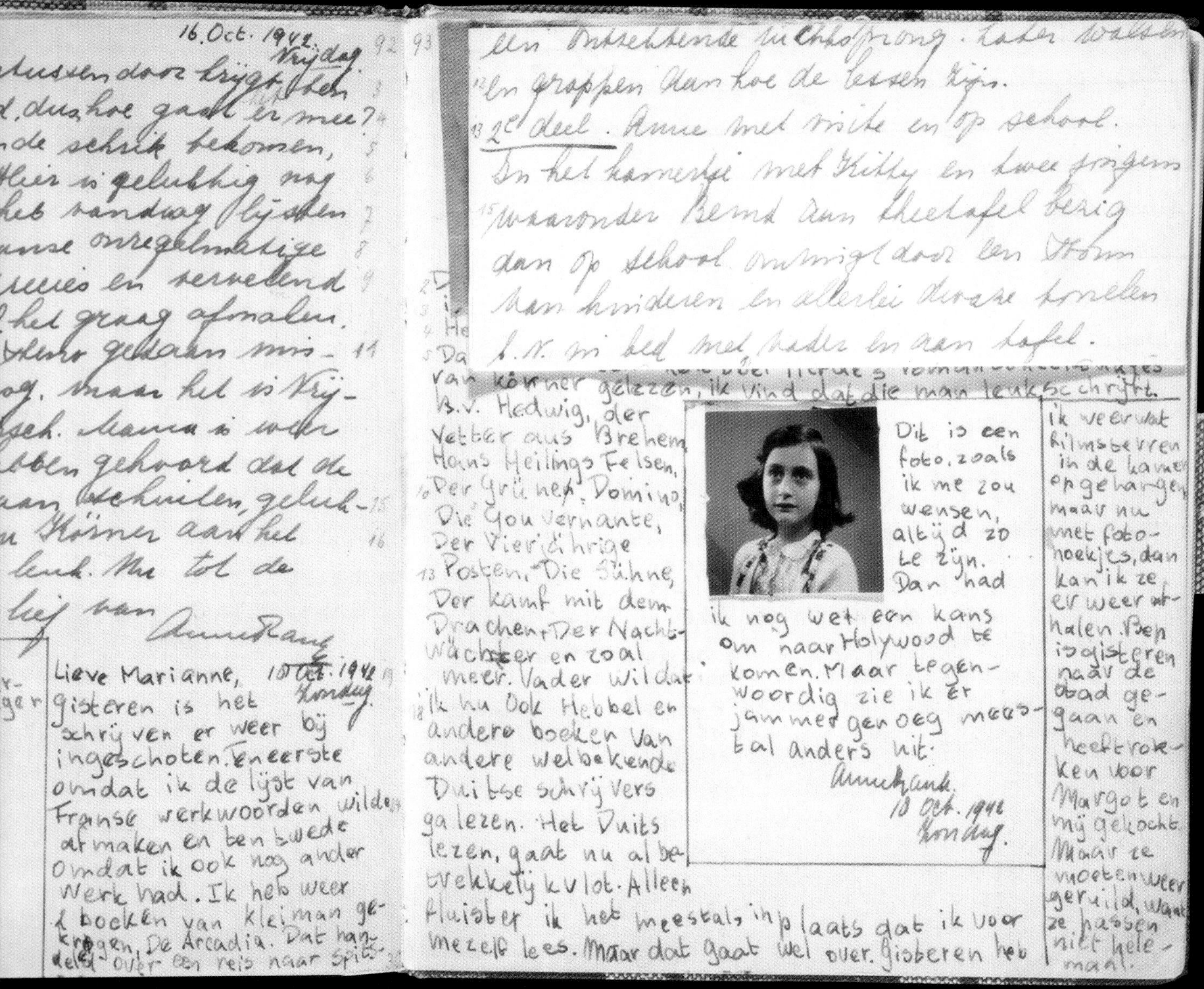

▶ parents for her 13th birthday, as an outlet for her feelings and to help pass the time. "Not being able to go outside upsets me more than I can say, and I'm terrified our hiding place will be discovered," Anne wrote in one entry.

Anne's words reflected her hope and love of writing. She decided she wanted to be a writer, and that her first book would be about life in the secret annex. She started rewriting her diary to be published after the war. On August 4, 1944, however, her worst fears came true. Someone had revealed their hiding place. Anne's diary was left behind when the police came to arrest them. She never finished rewriting it.

Anne died in the Bergen-Belsen concentration camp in March 1945, just weeks before British troops freed the camp. Her father was the only person from the secret annex who survived. When he returned to Amsterdam, he learned that one of his former office workers, Miep Gies, had saved Anne's diary. In 1947, Otto published it. Since then, Anne's diary has been translated into more than 65 languages.

In one of her most famous passages, Anne writes: "I still believe, in spite of everything, that people are truly good at heart." Anne's words of hope reached millions of readers. ■

The Frank family hid in an apartment in this building behind the office of Anne's father, Otto.

You Should Also Know ...

Miep Gies, courageous protector

• If not for Miep Gies, the world may have never known Anne Frank's story. Gies was one of a handful of Dutch citizens who protected the Franks from the Nazis. She risked her own life to try to save theirs. When the Franks were arrested, Gies found and saved Anne's diary. She gave it to Anne's father, Otto, after the war. "This is your daughter Anne's legacy," she told him.

The first printing of the book was called *The Secret Annex*. In the U.S., it is known as *The Diary of a Young Girl*. "I could not save Anne's life," Gies, who always resisted being called a hero, once said. "However, I did save her diary, and by that I could help her most important dreams to come true."

Who were the journalists who uncovered the Watergate scandal?

In the 1970s, two determined young journalists named **Bob Woodward** and **Carl Bernstein** came across what would be the biggest story of their careers—the Watergate scandal. The articles that resulted from their in-depth investigative reporting not only won them a Pulitzer Prize in 1973, but contributed to the downfall of a U.S. president.

On June 17, 1972, workers for President Richard M. Nixon's reelection campaign broke into rivals' offices at the Watergate hotel, in Washington, D.C. But at the time, no one knew who the burglars were working for. Woodward and Bernstein, who were assigned to cover the break-in for *The Washington Post*, did their own detective work. They met in secret with many insider sources to link the break-in—and the cover-up that followed—to top U.S. officials.

The thieves were trying to help the president win reelection to the White House. In November 1972, Nixon was reelected. Although he denied any involvement in Watergate, Woodward and Bernstein kept digging. As they uncovered more facts, the *Washington Post* and other news outlets kept the story in the public eye. More and more of Nixon's aides started to resign. Soon, people began to doubt the president.

Nixon's conversations in the White House had been recorded since 1971. In July 1974, the Supreme Court ordered the president to turn over 64 taped conversations

● **Bernstein (left) and Woodward work in the *Washington Post* newsroom in 1973.**

about Watergate. The tapes proved Nixon had known about the conspiracy. Congress began proceedings to formally charge the president with abusing his power to cover up the break-in. Nixon resigned from office on August 9, 1974. He was the first U.S. president to do so. Vice President Gerald Ford was sworn in as president that same day.

Woodward and Bernstein wrote a book about reporting on Watergate called *All the President's Men*, which was published while Nixon was still in office. It was later made into an Oscar-winning movie. Two years later, they released another book focusing on Nixon's last days as president, called *The Final Days*. ■

Who was the pilot who landed safely in the Hudson River in 2009?

● Sullenberger sits in a cockpit of a US Airways flight in 2009.

On January 15, 2009, **Captain Chesley "Sully" Sullenberger** was piloting a US Airways flight out of New York's LaGuardia Airport when a large flock of geese struck the plane, damaging both engines. The aircraft was coming down. Sullenberger had to think fast.

It was too risky to fly back to LaGuardia. Landing at another airport was also out of the question. With few options remaining, the veteran pilot prepared for an emergency landing on the frigid Hudson River, which runs alongside New York City. As he positioned the plane to glide into the water, Sullenberger came over the intercom and instructed everyone to "brace for impact." About 90 seconds later, the plane touched down safely in the river.

A rapid-rescue team met the plane and evacuated it. Sullenberger checked the cabin twice before deplaning himself. All 155 people onboard survived, and only one was seriously injured. Sullenberger, the first pilot in modern history to pull off a successful emergency water landing, became an instant celebrity.

The incident was dubbed Miracle on the Hudson. But Sullenberger's grace under pressure was less a miracle and more a result of his experience. The US Airways pilot was an aviation-safety expert with 29 years of commercial piloting under his belt. Before that, he had spent seven years in the United States Air Force. Despite his years of experience, Sullenberger called the landing a "startling shock" in an interview on *CBS This Morning*.

Congress later passed a resolution recognizing Sullenberger and his crew for their brave actions that day. He also earned the French Legion of Honor, France's highest award. In March 2010, Sullenberger retired from US Airways. He now travels the country giving talks about aviation safety. ■

● A rescue boat floats next to the US Airways plane that crashed into the Hudson River.

Navajo Code Talkers help relay messages to U.S. troops during World War II.

Who created a code that helped the Allies win World War II?

During World War II, the U.S. Marine Corps had a secret weapon that played a crucial role in helping the Americans win key battles. It wasn't a special tank or a powerful bomb—it was the **Navajo Code Talkers**.

Communication between allied troops on the battlefield is tremendously important in any war. It's even more critical that the communication is kept private from the enemy. But enemy forces in Japan kept cracking codes used by the U.S. military during World War II. The Americans needed a code that would be unbreakable. Former Army engineer Philip Johnston suggested they use the Navajo language.

Johnston had grown up around Navajo. His parents had served as missionaries on a Navajo reservation. He knew how complex the language could be to the untrained ear. Also, the Navajo language is not written, and only a handful of people outside the Navajo Nation could speak it. The Marines decided to take a chance on Johnston's proposal and approved a test program.

In the spring of 1942, the first 29 Navajo recruits came to Camp Elliott, near San Diego, California, to take part in a trial run. This group became known as the original Navajo Code Talkers. They developed the code by taking everyday words and substituting them for terms used in war. For instance, the Navajo names of birds were used for different types of planes. A special alphabet was created to spell out words that did not exist in the language.

More than 400 Navajo Code Talkers trained in the program. Their services were used in every major operation in the Pacific across all Marine divisions from 1942 to 1945. Using this unique code, the group communicated troop movements, battlefield tactics, and other crucial information via telephone and radio. The Japanese troops were never able to decipher the code. It gave the Marines a great advantage and saved the lives of countless American soldiers.

During the famed American invasion of the Japanese island of Iwo Jima, six Navajo Code Talkers worked nonstop in shifts throughout the ▶

Navajo Code Talkers take part in the 2009 Veterans Day parade in New York City.

first two days of the battle. They relayed more than 800 messages without any errors. Their skills earned them the respect of their comrades. Major Howard Connor was the signal officer of the Navajos at Iwo Jima. "Were it not for the Navajos, the Marines would never have taken Iwo Jima," Connor said.

Although they played a huge role in the war, the Navajo Code Talkers were largely unrecognized until 1968, when their mission was finally made public. Once the secret was out, the Code Talkers' heroism and contributions to the war effort were celebrated in books, films, and exhibits. In 1982, President Ronald Reagan declared August 14 "Navajo

Code Talkers Day." In 2001, President George W. Bush presented the four surviving members of the original 29 Navajo Code Talkers with one of the nation's highest honors—the Congressional Gold Medal. ■

You Should Also Know ...

Tuskegee Airmen, groundbreaking fighter pilots

• The Tuskegee Airmen were the first ever African-American fighter pilots for the U.S. military. They served in World War II. It was a time of racial discrimination. Black pilots and white pilots were forced to train separately. The black airmen trained in an airfield in Tuskegee, Alabama.

About 450 troops made up the original Tuskegee Airmen who saw action overseas. Hundreds more would train to be pilots.

The Tuskegee Airmen flew in more than 1,500 combat missions and rarely lost a bomber they escorted. In addition, they shot down more than a hundred enemy aircraft. For their brave service during WWII, the airmen received hundreds of medals. Their success also helped lead to the integration of the U.S. armed forces.

Who were the most decorated infantrymen in U.S. history?

Soldiers from the 442nd regiment stand at attention during a ceremony at Fort DeRussy, in Honolulu, Hawaii, in 1948.

The **442nd Regimental Combat Team** was a U.S. Army unit made up of Japanese Americans who fought during World War II. These volunteer soldiers valiantly battled enemy forces in Europe during the final years of the war. They did so despite the discrimination they faced back home. The 442nd remains the most decorated infantry regiment in U.S. military history.

On December 7, 1941, Japan attacked Pearl Harbor, a U.S. naval base in Hawaii. This brought the U.S. fully into the war. Two months later, President Franklin D. Roosevelt signed an executive order that permitted the forced relocation of 120,000 Japanese Americans to internment camps. The U.S. government banned Japanese-American citizens from serving in the military. When the ban was lifted, in 1943, a segregated unit known as the 442nd formed.

The soldiers of the 442nd quickly gained a reputation for their extraordinary bravery. Among the combat team's many accomplishments was the successful rescue of the Lost Battalion of the 141st Regiment. The 442nd saved the lives of 230 U.S. soldiers who had been trapped by German forces in the Vosges Mountains, in France. They also freed thousands of Jewish prisoners from sub-camps of the Dachau concentration camp complex, in Germany, in April 1945.

By the end of the war, the men of the 442nd had been honored with more than 18,000 awards. In 2010, President Barack Obama signed legislation bestowing the 442nd with the Congressional Gold Medal for their distinctive service in combat. ■

Who is the world's most famous pigeon?

● **This replica shows Cher Ami carrying a camera.**

Carrier pigeons delivered messages during World War I and World War II. Soldiers wrote down important information and strapped it to the legs of trained pigeons. The birds then flew back to home base to deliver their message to the commanders there. The U.S. Army Signal Corps in France enlisted 600 carrier pigeons for the war effort in 1917, during World War I.

One of these was **Cher Ami** (share ah-*mee*), French for *dear friend*. The bird successfully flew 12 urgent messages between U.S. troops in Verdun, France, in 1918. On his final mission, on October 4, 1918, a message he delivered saved the lives of nearly 200 soldiers on the front lines.

The message strapped to Cher Ami's leg was from Major Charles Whittlesey's Lost Battalion of the 77th Infantry Division. Major Whittlesey's unit, separated from other American forces, was surrounded by German troops. As Cher Ami rose into the air, he was shot through the breast and leg by enemy fire. But he still completed his mission. Not long after the message was delivered, the 194 soldiers in the battalion returned to safety behind American lines. Cher Ami was awarded a special French medal for his bravery and given a hero's welcome back home in the U.S. After his death, his preserved body went on display at the Smithsonian National Museum of American History, in Washington, D.C. ■

● The underdog U.S. Olympic hockey team celebrates after defeating the Soviet Union in 1980.

Who pulled off the Miracle on Ice at the 1980 Olympics?

On February 22, 1980, the **U.S. Olympic men's hockey team** completed one of the biggest and most unexpected wins in sports history at the Olympic Games in Lake Placid, New York. In a stunning victory, the underdog Americans defeated the heavily favored team from the Soviet Union (U.S.S.R.), 4–3. The Soviets, a dominant force in hockey, had taken the gold medal in the previous four Olympics.

At the time, tense relations between the U.S. and the U.S.S.R. set the stage for a dramatic matchup on the ice. In the days leading up to the big event, Team USA surprised everyone as they advanced toward the medal round. After tying Sweden 2–2 in the opening game, the U.S. team, which was made up of amateur and college players, went on to beat silver-medal favorites Czechoslovakia (check-us-slow-*vok*-ee-ah), Norway, Romania, and West Germany. ►

U.S.S.R. goalie Vladislav Tretiak (20) makes a save against Team USA's John Harrington (28) in the first period. The U.S would score four goals to win the Olympic matchup.

Finally, the Americans and the Soviets faced off on the ice. The teams were playing for a spot in the gold-medal match. The first period was a tight back-and-forth battle, with the U.S. tying it 2–2 with one second left in the period. The Soviets changed their goalie for the second period and dominated on offense, though they managed only one goal to take a 3–2 lead. But the tide turned in the third period, when the Americans scored two goals in two minutes, taking the lead for the first time in the game. U.S. goalie Jim Craig managed to fend off the nonstop barrage from the Soviets to keep the Americans firmly on top, 4–3.

As the clock ran out, the crowd erupted into cheers. Sportscaster Al Michaels had been calling the game for ABC. "Do you believe in miracles? YES!" he famously exclaimed as the final seconds ticked away.

The U.S. went on to capture the gold medal by beating Finland in the final round. But it's the win over the mighty Soviets—later known as the Miracle on Ice—that goes down as one of the greatest moments in sports history.

Sports Illustrated ran an image of the momentous occasion on its cover, without captions or headlines. There was no need for words—most of America had watched and celebrated the win. ■

Musicians Geldof (left) and Ure stand outside the London music studio where they recorded "Do They Know It's Christmas?" in 1984.

Who is the musician credited with organizing the Live Aid concerts?

In the mid-1980s, years of drought created a terrible famine, or food shortage, in Ethiopia. An estimated 1 million people died as a result of the hunger crisis. When news about the terrible situation spread around the world, international aid groups stepped in to help. Singer-songwriter **Bob Geldof** joined the effort.

The famed Irish rocker, along with musician Midge Ure, organized a supergroup of popular British and Irish recording artists that they called the Band Aid trust. The ensemble included big names like U2, Phil Collins, Sting, and Duran Duran. Together, the group recorded the single "Do They Know It's Christmas?" Proceeds from the song went toward famine relief in Ethiopia and surrounding countries. Upon its release, the track became the fastest-selling single in U.K. history. It raised more than $10 million for the cause.

The song inspired pop artists in the U.S. to form their own supergroup. Calling themselves "USA for Africa," stars, including Michael Jackson, Tina Turner, Stevie Wonder, Lionel Richie, and Cyndi Lauper, came together to record "We Are the World." The single raised $44 million for famine relief in Africa.

Geldof and company went on to produce a worldwide ▶

Geldof rocks the stage at the 1985 Live Aid charity concert in London, England.

▶ charity concert on July 13, 1985. Known as Live Aid, the main shows were held in Philadelphia, Pennsylvania, and London, England. More than 1 billion people in 110 countries watched on television. The program raised more than $125 million for famine relief.

Twenty years later, in July 2005, Geldof organized a series of Live 8 concerts in several countries. His goal was to spread awareness about global poverty and put pressure on world leaders to improve aid. When the Ebola crisis in West Africa reached its peak in 2014, Geldof once again reached out to fellow music megastars to help combat the deadly disease. As part of the 30th anniversary of "Do They Know It's Christmas?," Band Aid members old and new, from U2 to

One Direction, came together to raise funds for the fight against Ebola.

Geldof encourages others to step up. "There can be other Band Aids, there must be others, in new times, in different ways," he wrote in a Band Aid report. ■

You Should Also Know ...

Bono, activist and rock star

• U2 frontman Bono is another musical star known for using his celebrity for good. The Grammy-winning Irish rock musician has long been an outspoken advocate for social causes, including world hunger and AIDS.

Bono cofounded two nonprofit organizations, ONE and its sister organization, RED. ONE raises public awareness and works closely with activists and policy makers to combat poverty and preventable diseases, particularly in Africa. RED works to engage people in the fight to eliminate AIDS. Established in 2006, RED partners with companies, including Apple, Coca-Cola, and Starbucks, to develop RED-branded products. A portion of the profits from their sales goes to the Global Fund, which supports HIV/AIDS programs in Africa.

As of 2014, more than 55 million people had received much-needed care and services made possible by RED. Bono's philanthropic efforts have earned him several nominations for the Nobel Peace Prize.

Who traveled around the world alone for a newspaper assignment?

During the late 1800s, there were few women in journalism. A daring newspaper reporter named **Nellie Bly** led the charge to change that.

For Bly's first newspaper assignment in New York City, for Joseph Pulitzer's *New York World*, the 23-year-old went undercover to report on conditions at an insane asylum. Bly pretended to be a mentally ill patient for 10 days. Her story shed light on the many abuses faced by patients at the facility, which led to a number of much-needed reforms. That story, published in 1887, helped introduce a new kind of investigative reporting.

Bly had come to the *World* after two years at *The Pittsburgh Dispatch*, where her editors assigned her stories about flower shows and fashion. But the young reporter wanted to write about topics that were more hard-hitting and meaningful to her. She set off for the big city, leaving this note for her editor: "I'm off for New York. Look out for me. Bly."

Over the years, Bly exposed everything from the mistreatment of the poor to corruption in government. Many considered her a hero for the voiceless.

In 1889, Bly was sent by the *World* to break the fictional record set in Jules Verne's 1873 novel *Around the World in Eighty Days*. The fearless reporter departed New York City in November 1889, traveling alone, with only a small bag and a coat. She traveled around the globe by ship, horse, and various other methods, sending reports to her editors along the way. Seventy-two days, six hours, 11 minutes, and 14 seconds later, she successfully arrived back at home.

Bly married Robert Seaman in 1895. She quit journalism to help manage her husband's manufacturing company, and became president when he died in 1904. But hard times fell on the company, and Bly returned to her first love, journalism. She covered World War I in Europe, becoming the first female reporter to cover the conflict from the eastern front.

Upon returning home, Bly took a job at *The New York Evening Journal*. She wrote a column for the paper that focused on helping abandoned children. Bly was working for the *Journal* when she died of pneumonia in 1922. She was 57 years old. ■

This portrait of Bly was taken in 1890, the year after her trip around the world.

Index

Photo Credits

Back Cover: NASA/AFP/Getty Images; Max Mumby/Indigo/Getty Images; Walter Dhladhla/AFP/Getty Images; Rocky Widner/Getty Images
Pages 4–5: Ralph Morse/The Life Picture Collection/Getty Images; MyLoupe/UIG/Getty Images; Hulton Archive/Getty Images; Justin Sullivan/Getty Images; Doug Pensinger/Getty Images; Anne Frank Fonds Basel/Getty Images; Mario Tama/Getty Images; Al Tielemans/Sports Illustrated/Getty Images; Doring Kindersley/Getty Images; Max Mumby/Indigo/Getty Images; VOA/VIG/Getty Images; Mondadori Portfolio/Getty Images
Pages 6–7: Ralph Morse/The Life Picture Collection/Getty Images; Sports Studio Photos/Getty Images; Ed Lacey/Popperfoto/Getty Images; Michael Nichols/National Geographic/Getty Images; Keystone/Getty Images; Mondadori Portfolio/Getty Images; Transcendental Graphics/Getty Images
Page 8: The Print Collector
Page 9: NASA/AFP/Getty Images
Page 10: Blank Archives/Getty Images; SSPL/Getty Images
Page 12: The Collection Of The Supreme Court/MCT/Getty Images; Michael Ochs Archives/Getty Images
Page 13: CBS Photo Archive/Getty Images
Page 15: The Life Picture Collection/Getty Images
Page 16: Topical Press Agency/Getty Images
Page 17: The Dallas Morning News/MCT/Getty Images
Page 18: Bill Hogan/Chicago Tribune/MCT/Getty Images
Page 19: Lee Lockwood/The Life Picture Collection/Getty Images
Page 20: Mondadori Portfolio/Getty Images
Page 21: Keystone/Getty Images, Pictorial Parade/Getty Images
Pages 22: Ed Lacey/Popperfoto/Getty Images
Page 23: Walter Kelleher/NY Daily News Archives/Getty Images
Page 24: Allsport UK/Getty Images
Page 25: Jason Laveris/FilmMagic/Getty Images
Page 26: Transcendental Graphics/Getty Images
Page 27: Thomas D. McAvoy/The Life Picture Collection/Getty Images
Pages 28–29: Michael Nichols/National Geographic/Getty Images
Page 30: Sports Studio Photos/Getty Images
Page 31: Hulton Archive/Getty Images; National Baseball Hall Of Fame Library/Getty Images
Pages 32: Hulton Archive/Getty Images; Popperfoto/Getty Images
Page 33: Jessica Antolal/Getty Images
Page 34: Ralph Morse/The Life Picture Collection/Getty Images
Page 35: NASA/Getty Images
Page 36: Oxford Science Archive/Print Collector/Getty Images; Michael Rougier/The Life Picture Collection/Getty Images
Page 37: NASA/The Life Picture Collection/Getty Images
Pages 38–39: Hulton Archive/Getty Images
Page 40: Keystone/Getty Images
Page 41: Ken Regancamera 5/Getty Images
Pages 42–43: Walter Dhladhla/AFP/Getty Images; Thomas D. Mcavoy/The Life Picture Collection/Getty Images; VOA/VIG/Getty Images; Silver Screen Collection/Getty Images; Terry Smith/The Life Images Collection/Getty Images; Taylor Hill/Getty Images; Jean-Claude Francolon/Gamma-Rapho/Getty Images
Pages 44–45: VOA/VIG/Getty Images
Pages 46–47: Ann Ronan Pictures/Print Collector/Getty Images
Page 48: Michel Baret/Gamma-Rapho/Getty Images
Page 49: Taylor Hill/Getty Images
Pages 50–51: Walter Dhladhla/AFP/Getty Images
Page 52: Paul Weinberg/Gallo Images/Getty Images
Page 53: Foto24/Gallo Images/Getty Images
Page 54: Harry Langdon/Getty Images
Page 55: Silver Screen Collection/Getty Images
Pages 56–57: Francis Miller/The Life Picture Collection/Getty Images
Page 58: Donald Uhrbrock/The Life Picture Collection/Getty Images
Page 60: Oli Scarff/Getty Images
Pages 62–63: Keystone-France/Gamma/Getty Images
Page 64: Dick Loek/Toronto Star/Getty Images
Page 65: Jean-Claude Francolon/Gamma-Rapho/Getty Images
Page 66: Stock Montage/Getty Images
Page 67: MyLoupe/UIG/Getty Images; Photoquest/Getty Images
Page 68: CBS/Getty Images
Page 69: Terry Smith/The Life Images Collection/Getty Images
Page 70: Underwood Archives/Getty Images
Page 71: William Philpott/Getty Images
Page 72: Bob Costa/NY Daily News Archive/Getty Images
Page 73: Ann Ronan Pictures/Print Collector/Getty Images
Page 74: Thomas D. Mcavoy/The Life Picture Collection/Getty Images
Page 75: Hulton Archive/Getty Images; London Express/Getty Images
Pages 76–77: Silver Screen Collection/Getty Images; Jason Tanner/UNHCR/Getty Images; Michael Ochs Archives/Getty Images; Timothy A. Clary/AFP/Getty Images; Steve Sands/GC Images/Getty Images; Kevin Winter/Getty Images for IHeart Media; Hulton Archive/Getty Images
Pages 78–79: Fred Duval/Getty Images
Page 80: Kevin Winter/Getty Images for IHeart Media
Page 81: Harry Hammond/V&A Images/Getty Images
Page 82: Stuart C. Wilson/Getty Images
Page 83: Albert L. Ortega/Getty Images
Page 84: Timothy A. Clary/AFP/Getty Images; Doug Jones/Portland Press Herald/Getty Images
Page 85: Vera Anderson/WireImage/Getty Images
Pages 86–87: Kevin Mazur/Getty Images for DirecTV; The Life Picture Collection/Getty Images
Page 88: Hulton Archive/Getty Images
Page 89: Michael Ochs Archives/Getty Images
Page 90: Kris Connor/Getty Images
Page 91: Hulton Archive/Getty Images
Page 92: Steve Sands/GC Images/Getty Images
Page 93: Larry Busacca/Getty Images
Page 94: Apic/Getty Images
Page 95: Hulton Archive/Getty Images; Jun Sato/Wireimage/Getty Images
Page 96: Silver Screen Collection/Getty Images
Page 97: Rich Polk/Getty Images For MSN Wonderwall
Page 98: Vince Bucci/Getty Images
Page 99: John Bryson/The Life Images Collection/Getty Images
Pages 100–101: Jason Tanner/UNHCR/Getty Images
Page 102: J. Tanner/UNHCR/Getty Images, UNICEF/Hulton Archive/Getty Images
Page 103: Max Mumby/Indigo/Getty Images
Pages 104–105: David Paul Morris/Bloomberg/Getty Images; Charles Trainor/The Life Images Collection/Getty Images; Andreas Feininger/The Life Picture Collection/Getty Images; Jemal Countess/WireImage for Time Inc./Getty Images; Walter Carone/Paris Match/Getty Images; Volkmarki Wentzel/National Geographic/Getty Images; Fred Stein/Getty Images
Page 106: Justin Sullivan/Getty Images
Page 107: Ralph Morse/The Life Picture Collection/Getty Images
Page 108: David Paul Morris/Bloomberg/Getty Images
Page 109: Stock Montage/Getty Images
Pages 110–111: Frederick M. Brown/Getty Images
Page 112: Paul E. Alers/NASA/Getty Images; Jon Brenneis/The Life Picture Collection/Getty Images
Page 113: Universal History Archive/Getty Images
Page 116: Chris Ware/Keystone Features/Getty Images
Page 117: Oxford Science Archive/Getty Images; Keystone Features/Getty Images
Page 118: Apic/Getty Images
Page 119: Getty Images
Page 120: Walter Carone/Paris Match/Getty Images
Page 121: Lipnitzki/Roger Viollet/Getty Images
Page 122: Express/Getty Images
Page 123: Andreas Feininger/The Life Picture Collection/Getty Images
Page 124: Doring Kindersley/Getty Images; Science Source/Getty Images
Page 125: Alberto E. Rodriguez/Getty Images
Pages 126–127: Fred Stein/Getty Images
Page 128: Archive Photos/Getty Images
Page 129: Charles Trainor/The Life Images Collection/Getty Images
Page 130: Archive Photos/Getty Images
Page 131: Popperfoto/Getty Images, Alberto Pizzoli/AFP/Getty Images
Pages 132–133: Jemal Countess/WireImage for Time Inc./Getty Images
Pages 134–35: Albert Eisenstaedt/The Life Picture Collection/Getty Images
Page 136: Volkmar K. Wentzel/National Geographic/Getty Images
Page 137: Ben Hider/Getty Images; Jack Mitchell/Getty Images
Pages 138–139: Al Tielemans/Sports Illustrated/Getty Images; Doug Pensinger/Getty Images; Barry Gossage/NBAE/Getty Images; David E. Klutho/Sports Illustrated/Getty Images; Vincent Laforet/Getty Images; Hulton Archive/Getty Images; Richard Meek/Sports Illustrated/Getty Images
Pages 140–141: Brian Babineau/NBAE/Getty Images
Page 142: NBC/NBCU Photo Bank/Getty Images
Page 143: Richard Meek/Sports Illustrated/Getty Images
Page 144: Hulton Archive/Getty Images, Pascal Le Segretain/Getty Images
Page 145: Vincent Laforet/Getty Images
Page 146: Doug Pensinger/Getty Images
Page 147: Mike Powell/AllSport/Getty Images
Page 148: John Leyba/The Denver Post/Getty Images
Page 149: David Madison/Getty Images
Pages 150–151: Glyn Kirk/AFP/Getty Images
Page 152: Barry Gossage/NBAE/Getty Images
Page 153: Fabrice Coffrini/AFP/Getty Images
Page 154: Al Tielemans/Sports Illustrated/Getty Images
Page 155: Nick Laham/Getty Images
Page 156: Ezra Shaw/Getty Images
Page 157: Steve Powell/AllSport/Getty Images
Page 158: Transcendental Graphics/Getty Images
Page 159: Louis Oeyen/Western Reserve Historical Society/Getty Images
Page 160: Mark Rucker/Transcendental Graphics/Getty Images
Page 161: Pictorial Parade/Getty Images
Page 162: David E. Klutho/Sports Illustrated/Getty Images
Page 163: Underwood Archives/Getty Images
Pages 164–165: Andrew Theodorakis/NY Daily News; Paul Slade/Paris Match/Getty Images; Larry Ellis/Express Newspapers/Getty Images; Stephanie De Sakutin/AFP/Getty Images; Heinz Kluetmeier/Sports Illustrated/Getty Images; Anne Frank Fonds Basel/Getty Images; Mario Tama/Getty Images
Pages 166–167: Anne Frank Fonds Basel/Getty Images
Page 168: Anne Frank Fonds Basel/Getty Images; AFP/Getty Images
Page 169: Anne Frank Fonds Basel/Getty Images
Pages 170–171: Paul Slade/Paris Match/Getty Images
Page 172: Andrew Theodorakis/NY Daily News Archive/Getty Images
Page 173: Jerritt Clark/Getty Images
Pages 174–175: Fotosearch/Getty Images
Page 176: Mario Tama/Getty Images
Page 177: Afro American Newspapers/Getty Images
Page 178: Eliot Elisofon/The Life Picture Collection/Getty Images
Page 179: Paul J. Richards/AFP/Getty Images
Pages 180–181: Focus On Sport/Getty Images
Pages 182–183: Heinz Kluetmeier/Sports Illustrated/Getty Images
Pages 184–185: Larry Ellis/Express Newspapers/Getty Images
Page 186: Steve Rapport/Photoshot/Getty Images; Phil Dent/Redferns/Getty Images
Page 187: Stephanie De Sakutin/AFP/Getty Images
Page 189: Interim Archives/Getty Images

WHO WAS THE BRITISH PRIME MINISTER KNOWN AS THE IRON LADY? WHO HELPED BRING TH
E SELF-MADE MILLIONAIRE? WHO COFOUNDED APPLE AND TRANSFORMED THE DIGITAL WORLD?
LIES WIN WORLD WAR II? WHO WAS THE FIRST WOMAN TO FLY SOLO ACROSS THE ATLANTIC? WH
LITIES? WHO CREATED TWITTER? WHO SAID HE COULD "FLOAT LIKE A BUTTERFLY, STING LIKE
N AMERICAN TO WIN THE U.S. OPEN AND WIMBLEDON? WHOSE BOOK LAUNCHED THE MODERN
BLY LINE? WHO BEGAN HIS MUSICAL CAREER AT AGE 4 BY IMPERSONATING ELVIS? WHO IS TH
ECAME A VOICE FOR HOLOCAUST VICTIMS WHEN HER DIARY WAS PUBLISHED? WHO WERE THE FI
I? WHO IS THE OSCAR-WINNING DIRECTOR BEHIND JAWS, E.T., AND INDIANA JONES? WHO WON
? WHO PIONEERED THE CUBIST ART MOVEMENT? WHO PUT U.S. WOMEN'S SOCCER ON THE MAP?
N AND PRODUCE HER OWN TALK SHOW? WHOSE LEADERSHIP SHAPED THE CIVIL-RIGHTS MOVEN
VO NOBEL PRIZES? WHO WAS KNOWN AS THE SULTAN OF SWAT? WHO TRAVELED AROUND THE W
EST PERSON TO RECEIVE THE NOBEL PEACE PRIZE? WHO ARE THE TENNIS-STAR SISTERS WHO
NG? WHO WAS THE FIRST POLISH CARDINAL TO BE ELECTED POPE? WHO IS THE HOLLYWOOD AC
RST AFRICAN-AMERICAN GYMNAST TO WIN THE OLYMPIC INDIVIDUAL ALL-AROUND EVENT? WHO
N? WHO WROTE THE CAT IN THE HAT? WHO WAS THE KING OF ROCK 'N' ROLL? WHO IS THE SC
ENT OF THE U.S.? WHO CREATED THE MUPPETS? WHO DEVELOPED THE THEORY OF RELATIVITY?
JUSTICE? WHO LED BRITAIN TO VICTORY DURING WORLD WAR II? WHO DISCOVERED THE DOUB
AT THE 1980 OLYMPICS? WHO WERE THE FIRST PEOPLE TO WALK ON THE MOON? WHOSE FOUND
OF POP? WHO CHANGED THE FASHION INDUSTRY? WHO BROKE MAJOR-LEAGUE BASEBALL'S C
IOUS? WHO FOUNDED YOUTUBE? WHO WAS THE YOUNGEST NHL CAPTAIN TO WIN A STANLEY CU
E OF ALL TIME? WHO WAS SOUTH AFRICA'S FIRST BLACK PRESIDENT? WHO WAS THE MAN BEH
ONSIDERED THE GREATEST FEMALE ATHLETE OF THE 20TH CENTURY? WHO LED THE MOVEMENT
CUBAN MISSILE CRISIS? WHO WAS THE FIRST WOMAN TO RUN A MAJOR TELEVISION STUDIO?
R FAMOUS FOR HER SELF-PORTRAITS? WHO WAS ISRAEL'S FIRST FEMALE PRIME MINISTER? W
SPEAK SOFTLY AND CARRY A BIG STICK?" WHO REDEFINED THE ROLE OF THE FIRST LADY? WHO
POTTER SERIES? WHO IS THE SCIENTIST BEST KNOWN FOR STUDYING BLACK HOLES? WHO HA
WHO REDEFINED THE ROLE OF THE FIRST LADY? WHO WAS THE BRITISH PRIME MINISTER KNO
OOK? WHO BECAME THE COUNTRY'S FIRST FEMALE SELF-MADE MILLIONAIRE? WHO COFOUND
GAMES? WHO CREATED A CODE THAT HELPED THE ALLIES WIN WORLD WAR II? WHO WAS THE F
HO WAS A LEADING CHAMPION FOR PEOPLE WITH DISABILITIES? WHO CREATED TWITTER? WHO SA
ATERGATE SCANDAL? WHO WAS THE FIRST AFRICAN AMERICAN TO WIN THE U.S. OPEN AND WIMB
IE HULK? WHO INVENTED THE MOVING ASSEMBLY LINE? WHO BEGAN HIS MUSICAL CAREER AT
TBALL PHENOM KNOWN AS KING JAMES? WHO BECAME A VOICE FOR HOLOCAUST VICTIMS WHE
REFUSAL TO CHANGE SEATS CHANGED THE NATION? WHO IS THE OSCAR-WINNING DIRECTOR BE
IE FIRST AMERICAN TO ORBIT THE EARTH? WHO PIONEERED THE CUBIST ART MOVEMENT? WHO
RTS? WHO WAS THE FIRST WOMAN TO OWN AND PRODUCE HER OWN TALK SHOW? WHOSE LEAI
I? WHO WAS THE ONLY WOMAN TO WIN TWO NOBEL PRIZES? WHO WAS KNOWN AS THE SULTAN C
QUEEN OF JAZZ? WHO WAS THE YOUNGEST PERSON TO RECEIVE THE NOBEL PEACE PRIZE?
CANS MASTER THE ART OF FRENCH COOKING? WHO WAS THE FIRST POLISH CARDINAL TO BE ELE
EVELOPED PENICILLIN? WHO WAS THE FIRST AFRICAN-AMERICAN GYMNAST TO WIN THE OLYMPI
FIGHT FOR INDEPENDENCE FROM BRITAIN? WHO WROTE THE CAT IN THE HAT? WHO WAS THE
E THE FIRST AFRICAN-AMERICAN PRESIDENT OF THE U.S.? WHO CREATED THE MUPPETS? WHO D
IE FIRST HISPANIC U.S. SUPREME COURT JUSTICE? WHO LED BRITAIN TO VICTORY DURING WO